Teaching Notes

on Piano Exam Pieces

2017 & 2018

Grades 1–8

Timothy Barratt

Samantha Carrasco

Sharon Gould

Margaret Murray McLeod

Nicholas Oliver

Mark Tanner

Anthony Williams

ABRSM

First published in 2016 by ABRSM (Publishing) Ltd, a wholly owned subsidiary of ABRSM, 24 Portland Place, London W1B 1LU, United Kingdom

© 2016 by The Associated Board of the Royal Schools of Music

ISBN 978 1 84849 897 6
AB 3838

A CIP catalogue for this book is available from The British Library.

Cover by Kate Benjamin & Andy Potts
Printed in England by Page Bros (Norwich) Ltd, on materials from sustainable sources

CONTENTS

FOREWORD

by ABRSM Chief Examiner, John Holmes

Choosing new pieces is always exciting – rather like setting out on a journey to somewhere you haven't been before. As a teacher, you are presented with an opportunity to match your students' skills and preferences to the right music for them, while also making use of your expertise to ensure the right level of challenge to encourage the development of technique and musicianship. This book is intended to help guide you in making good decisions, together with your student, about which pieces will work most successfully. It sets out to provide useful insights into each piece, which we hope will support you and your students on your teaching and learning journeys.

The expert contributors are all piano teachers with a wealth of examining experience. They are able to draw from their knowledge and understanding gained in each of these contexts to provide valuable hints and tips, as well as helpful advice on how to develop the musical relationship that links composer, score and performer.

In fact, the choice of piece is only the first in an almost never-ending series of choices which becomes the learning journey I mentioned at the beginning. Whether it's Chopin, Clementi or Copland, Skryabin, Shchedrin or Schumann, a whole range of decisions – conscious and subconscious – will need to be made in order for the developing pianist to arrive at their destination, in this case, the exam performance. Tempo, touch, fingering, pedalling, phrasing ... the list of choices goes on, so perhaps it would be helpful here to talk about how the decision-making process might be approached.

It is crucial to note that there is no 'ABRSM way' of playing any of our piano exam pieces, although of course there *is* an 'ABRSM way' of assessing how they are played. This is by considering the overall musical outcome – in effect, the cumulative result of all the various musical and technical decisions that will have been made in preparing the performance. For example, ABRSM examiners don't assess fingering, but we do comment on and evaluate its effects, such as evenness of tone or regularity of delivery, which are so often partly the result of fingering choices. Examiners are listening and looking for the degree of skill a candidate shows in controlling elements of pitch, time, tone, shape and performance, which develop gradually during their learning and practice prior to the exam. It is these elements that form the basis of our marking criteria, which are used by examiners in all ABRSM practical graded exams.

Between them, the ABRSM scores, recordings and *Teaching Notes* are intended to open a variety of doorways to interpretation. There may well be differences between what the scores imply, what the recordings present and what these *Teaching Notes* recommend – but in reality they do not so much contradict as complement each other. We would like to encourage you to inspire your students to play with creativity and individuality, leading them to achieve successful performances that suit and reflect their particular skills, strengths and enthusiasms.

That's the excitement of every musical journey – there will always be a variety of routes to a successful musical result, and our examiners do not mark candidates according to any particular one; instead they judge the combined effectiveness of the various musical performance decisions you and your student have made, taken as a whole. This means that every candidate can play to their strengths, not only in their particular choice of pieces, but also in the way that they interpret them. For example, there is a range of tempos – a 'bandwidth' of speeds – at which any given piece can successfully be played. For some pieces this will be wider than for others, but even where a metronome mark is given, there is usually room for some flexibility of approach. The examiner will not be marking the speed of playing absolutely or in isolation, but rather in conjunction with other elements of performance, such as note accuracy and rhythmic character. The right tempo choice for each student is best determined as part of a comfortable balance between the speed and other elements, so that one thing is not sacrificed to another – precision sacrificed to speed, for example.

Other decisions to be made include phrasing, ornament realization, whether to add dynamics, play straight or swing quavers, and when to use the pedal. The examiner will be assessing the overall musical outcome, rather than the strict observance of any printed pedal indications, which means that these may be adapted or omitted to suit the needs of the individual. However, it is important to bear in mind the strengths of your student. Therefore, pieces whose full musical effect is heavily reliant on pedalling (whether marked in the music or not) might best be avoided if appropriate pedalling cannot be managed.

It is worth reiterating that using the ABRSM marking criteria (which can be found online and within the Piano syllabus), examiners will assess the musical outcome heard on the day: the musical effectiveness of the piano playing in the exam room. The best results will arise from a well-judged match between each individual candidate's piano skills, and the particular demands of the chosen piece.

Candidates can choose the order in which they play their three pieces, and whether to start the exam with these or another section – scales, for example. Once again there is no single right way; as with so much of the musical learning journey leading to performance, the exam itself starts with a decision!

We do hope that you will feel excited and inspired by the wonderful range of musical possibilities open to you and your students within the 2017 & 2018 ABRSM Piano syllabus. Spanning around 400 years of composition, whether it's Kabalevsky or Khachaturian, there is truly something for everyone to embark upon and enjoy.

ABOUT THE AUTHORS

All of the authors have a wealth of teaching and examining experience, which covers a wide variety of musical styles. Each author has contributed to a mixture of grades and lists. The initials shown above each teaching note can be used to identify its author.

TIMOTHY BARRATT ARAM GRSM LRAM ARCM LMusTCL

Tim studied at the Royal Academy of Music and in Paris with Vlado Perlemuter. As a solo pianist, accompanist and chamber music player, he has performed extensively throughout the UK and abroad. He has considerable experience of teaching at all levels, as Head of Keyboard at Dulwich College from 1992–2016, and as a lecturer and vocal coach at the RAM and Trinity College of Music. He is an ABRSM examiner, trainer, moderator and international presenter.

SAMANTHA CARRASCO PhD MMus BMus(Hons) ARCM

Samantha studied at the Royal College of Music and performs regularly as a soloist, accompanist, orchestral player and chamber musician. She teaches piano at the University of Southampton and Winchester College and is an examiner, trainer, moderator and presenter for the ABRSM, nationally and internationally, in classical, jazz and diplomas. She has broadcast on Radio 3 and Classic FM and plays orchestral piano with the Bournemouth Symphony Orchestra.

SHARON GOULD MA ARCM (SG)

Sharon read music at Cambridge University, and has performed extensively as a harpsichord soloist and Baroque orchestral director in the UK and internationally. As a pianist, she performs in a piano duo, as an accompanist and as a chamber musician. She has taught at the Royal College of Music Junior Department, at Chetham's School of Music and at the Royal Northern College of Music; her former students include several international award winners. Sharon is an ABRSM examiner, trainer and moderator.

MARGARET MURRAY McLEOD ARAM FTCL LRAM ARCM

Margaret studied piano and composition at the Royal Academy of Music. As well as performing as a soloist and accompanist, she has many years' experience of teaching at all levels. From 1972 she trained student teachers and performers at Edinburgh Napier University, where she was Senior Lecturer for Performance Studies until 1997. Her work as a lecturer, examiner and adjudicator has taken her worldwide, and in 2014 she was appointed a Regional Organiser for the European Piano Teachers Association.

NICHOLAS OLIVER GRSM LRAM PGRNCM

Nicholas combines the role of Head of Accompaniment at Chetham's School of Music with freelance performing, teaching, examining and writing. He studied at the Royal Academy of Music, and as a postgraduate at the Royal Northern College of Music, later returning to teach at the Junior RNCM. He is a grade and diploma examiner for ABRSM and is on the training panel. As a director of The Commonwealth Resounds, a musical charity, he has led music education projects in several countries.

MARK TANNER PhD Hon.BC MA FTCL FRSA

Mark received his doctorate from the Birmingham Conservatoire. Recitals include London's Wigmore Hall, alongside 300 appearances on cruise ships. He has recorded extensively and broadcast on BBC Radio 3 and Classic FM. Mark is an ABRSM examiner, trainer and international presenter, having undertaken 30 tours to five continents. Publications include 60 volumes of compositions and arrangements for Edition Peters and Spartan Press. Mark teaches at Chetham's International Piano Summer School, and his 'Masterclass' articles feature in *Pianist* magazine.

ANTHONY WILLIAMS MMus Dip.RAM GRSM LRAM

Anthony has an active performing, teaching and adjudicating career in the UK and abroad and is currently Head of Keyboard and Instrumental Music at Radley College, Oxfordshire. As a piano specialist he regularly presents teacher support lecture-recitals and is an examiner (jazz and classical), trainer and moderator for ABRSM. He is the compiler of *Fingerprints* and the *Best of Grade* series for piano, and editor of *Simply Classics* (all published by Faber Music).

HOW TO USE THIS BOOK

In the newly revised *Teaching Notes*, every note contains teaching ideas relating to three areas of learning: musical context, technical challenges, and performance and interpretation.

Syllabus list numbers and author initials are shown at the top of each piece, either side of the composer name and piece title, for example:

 **J. C. Bach** Aria in F (TB)

MUSICAL CONTEXT

The first section explains where the piece fits within the world of music, and introduces the distinctive features of the piece. Genre, period, structure and style may be mentioned here, as well as information about the composer. You might also find suggestions of music to listen to, which will help your student gain familiarity with the musical context.

TECHNICAL CHALLENGES

In this section the trickiest corners of the piece are identified and suggestions to help tackle them are provided. Alternative ornament realizations and fingering may appear here, as well as practice ideas to help with agility and coordination.

PERFORMANCE AND INTERPRETATION

This section focuses on communicating the music with style and personality. These elements can help turn an accurate performance into one with real artistic value.

General advice about interpreting the score, hand stretch, pedalling and repeats can be found in the Piano syllabus, under 'Piano requirements and information'.

Share learning tips and discuss the latest pieces with the piano teaching community via ABRSM Teacher Views.

Find out more at www.abrsm.org/pianonotes

GRADE 1

A:1   J. C. Bach   Aria in F   (TB)

One can imagine this gifted child composer performing his piece to entertain family, no doubt earning the praise of his distinguished father. The title 'Aria' suggests a cantabile style of playing, its minim pulse helping the lines to flow gently, without undue accentuation. It was probably written for either the harpsichord or clavichord, and its rounded phrases have a natural sense of elegance and balance.

A few twists and turns in both hands may need care. Locating the changes of position in advance of playing will prevent any hiatus, especially when both hands shift together in bar 11, and confident placement of the thumb will ensure that the LH shapes flow reliably. Omitting the trill initially in practice will establish the pace of the underlying crotchets; an alternative for the trill than the marked triplets would be to play eight semiquavers, which may be easier to coordinate.

Each of the four main phrases has its own tonal rise and fall. Dropping back sufficiently at the *mp*, taking care not to add an extra beat at the double bar-line, provides definition to the midway point, and in bar 11 either a *subito f* or one prepared by a crescendo works well. Detached crotchets provide an airiness to the texture, contrasting with the slurs, and the light upbeat crotchets propel the starts of phrases across the bar-line.

A:2   Anon.   Canaries   (TB)

Here one might imagine an Elizabethan lutenist, dressed in their finery, playing this piece in the chamber of a grand house, perhaps to entertain a lover. The dotted figures give a dance-like skip to the rhythmic pulse, while a crisp, light touch will emulate the clarity and precision of attack of the lute. The changes in dynamic, usually every two bars, add definition to the phrases, all of which are of equal length.

Although notes remain within the same five-finger shape for more than half of the piece, a small separation before the end of bars 12 and 16 will help to prepare new hand positions. The dotted figures will maintain rhythmic poise if the dotted quaver is full-length, and some initial LH practice may be needed to coordinate the faster notes. The two ornaments should flow without any rhythmic distortion; young students often respond to made-up words to fit such rhythmic challenges.

A mixture of staccato and slurs in the RH is a stylish option here, while light offbeat notes, taking particular care with thumb notes, will convey the buoyancy of a two-in-a-bar dance. Extending the demands of Grade 1 aural test D

1

to incorporate distinguishing between the four dynamic levels of this piece may be a good starting point in creating an effectively varied tonal range.

[A:3] **Verdi** La donna è mobile (The woman is fickle) (TB)

Although the singer appears to bemoan the flighty character of women, with their changes of mood as unpredictable as a feather blowing in the breeze, the boldness and confidence of the music leaves one in little doubt about his affections. Students may imagine, or, better still, listen to the full-bodied tone of an operatic tenor singing this aria – larger than life, yet sensitive to all the contrasts of nuance suggested by the text.

Well-defined rhythms, with accurate-length semiquavers in the dotted figures and evenly spaced triplets, will underpin performance. Coordination of the contrasting articulation between the hands in bars 1–8 may need practice and care is needed to give rests their full value. Slightly shortening the note preceding a change of position will allow the hands to locate the new notes without loss of fluency.

Shapely RH phrases, as if sung, convey the vocal character of this arrangement. Quick-fire contrasts of tone and articulation reflect the ever-shifting moods, as they alternate flirtatiously between laughter and tears. Time seems suspended at the *rall.* in bar 13, which offers a truly operatic moment, before progress is resumed at the *a tempo*. Light thumb notes in the LH will establish the one-in-a-bar swagger and impetus, while accents on the second beat at bars 10 and 12 offer a rhythmic twist.

[A:4] **S. Arnold** Giga (TB)

The Giga (or 'Jig' in English) with its characteristic compound rhythms was a favourite dance movement in the seventeenth and eighteenth centuries. A two-in-a-bar rhythmic feel, without undue emphasis on individual quavers, will capture the athleticism and brilliance of this joyful music. However, imagining the speed of the quavers before playing will stop your student from playing at a tempo which cannot be maintained in the exam.

Using the tips of all fingers, lifting each one cleanly, will ensure clear articulation of the quavers, with no overlap of sounds. Joins between bars should be seamless and the leap at bar 5 needs swift movement, locating the next hand position in advance to prevent a hiatus. Ornaments, although not obligatory, add stylistic interest, provided that they fit neatly with the LH quavers without distorting the rhythm.

Forte tone at the outset which is clear, rather than heavy, will immediately capture the brightness of C major. Each four-bar cascading pattern has its own shape and inflection, and lightly detached LH dotted crotchets and full-valued rests add buoyancy. The *p* at bar 9, with its quaver imitation between the hands, provides a welcome contrast. Coordination of the hands needs care here in order to convey the contrasts of articulation. The return to f may be sudden or may follow a preparatory crescendo in the previous bar – either works well.

A:5 Beethoven Air (TB)

The bold, confident character of this folk-like piece shows many hallmarks of Beethoven's style. Phrasing is clear-cut, consisting of four- or two-bar units, each with its own dynamic level, and a well-judged tempo will allow poise to the phrasing while maintaining the sense of flow and airiness. This piece is taken from a collection of National Airs with Variations, and was first published in 1820.

Some repetition of note patterns is an aid to learning, although the twists and turns in the LH may need special practice. Coordination of slurred and detached RH notes with smooth LH lines is likely to be the main challenge. Gently releasing the second note of slurs gives elegance to the phrasing, and clear dotted rhythms, with the semiquavers sufficiently short, will highlight the change of mood in the second half.

Singing the melody, breathing at ends of phrases, is the most effective way to understand the structure, while helping to develop aural skills. Confident students might even explore 'call and response' with their teacher. The predominantly gentle mood of the first half is created by graceful inflection of tone and light repeated notes. Appoggiaturas, sensitively tapered, add elegance to ends of phrases, and a contrast between mf and mp offers variety. Strongly articulated repeated notes announce the change of character at bar 9. Separating the two-bar phrases here, as if breathing, will provide definition, especially if the mp is sufficiently quiet.

A:6 Gillock A Stately Sarabande (TB)

Although written in the twentieth century, this Baroque-style piece evokes the atmosphere and elegance of a former age. One might imagine finely attired courtiers moving gracefully within an elegant ballroom. A stately tempo will reflect the formality of the dance, and avoiding overemphasis on each beat will allow the phrases to flow easily.

Although the LH mostly plays an accompanying role, its cello-like solo phrases at bar 17 offer scope for firm, expressive playing; projecting this needs a firmer touch, feeling to the base of the keys. Phrasing between the hands is usually matched, although confident coordination is needed to show the rests in the middle section. Terminating the dotted minims early at ends of phrases will allow time to move position without distorting the pulse.

The clear-cut ternary structure, with its contrasting central portion sandwiched between identical outer sections, may provide a starting point for discussing form. The natural arch of the opening four-bar phrases creates its own shape, and one-bar slurs give further definition. Gracefully tapered phrase endings add charm and gesture, with echo effects created by clearly differentiated *f*/*p* contrasts. From bar 9 the terraced dynamics, a stylistic feature of Baroque music, draw attention to the descending sequences. Well-controlled tone, gauging the diminuendo over 8 bars, will achieve this effect, and accents in bars 17 and 19 highlight suspensions over the bar-line.

B:1   Joan Last   Bouncing Billy

Playfully weaving between the hands is a fabulous, jokey melody full of playground fun and nursery-rhyme simplicity. It's a game of catch-me-if-you-can, with sudden shifts from LH to RH, and a journey through chromatic ambiguity.

Central to its effectiveness is a confident control of the articulation, and quick adaptability, moving, for example, from the legato phrasing of the opening to a hopping, small-stepped staccato. A lightness of touch will help, with the short notes played from close to the key's surface with a light bounce at the wrist or flick of the finger. The fingers need conditioning to create the right sound every time, the melody always projected and all accompanying notes in the background. Highlighting the melodic line on the score will help identify the important notes. In the opening bar, for instance, the F in the LH should be softer than the A in the RH but its following C projected as part of the melodic line.

A successful performance will convey the bold dynamic contrasts; a rude *f* (bar 21) is followed by a cheeky *dim.*, with a mischievous *molto rit.* and long pause. The suggested tempo marking of ♩. = *c*.60 may seem cautious but it enables an enthusiastic, roguish *molto cresc.* and *poco stringendo* in the final line. The *senza rit.* should be taken literally – a triumphant winning gesture.

B:2   Bryan Kelly   Gypsy Song

A melancholy story is unveiled in this beautiful song. It's a vocal duet between the hands, and the tale is projected through bold, dynamic shaping and detailed articulation. Understanding the musical shape of each 'sung' part (imagining words for it) and suggesting the breaths a singer might take will help in developing the most appropriate sounds and nuances.

Bars 17–24 may need technical work as the LH has to project above the RH; separate practice including the expressive detail will encourage an independence of line and help with coordination before the hands are put together. A warm, blended cantabile tone between notes (using a true physical legato) with a slight lift at the end will give the impression of a single breath for each phrase.

The tenuto marks in bar 9 are not accents but might suggest single, important words in the tale. The two narrators here, over bars 9–12, have a different phrasing, which your student should try to convey. Communicating the dynamic contrast of the tearful echo in bars 15–16 is also important; and although not marked, a reflective slowing of the tempo in bar 16 before the tune enters in the LH would work well. The final two bars enticingly imply a repeat of the previous two, but instead end on a poignant tierce de Picardie, the lovely C♯ anticipated by a gentle, resigned *rit.*

B:3 Trad. French Dans la forêt lointaine (In the Distant Forest)

There is colourful storytelling in this song-like piece. Two cuckoos playfully answer each other, flying around, one distant and one close by. The melody either side of the calls seems to sing of their antics, mimicking their distance in the matching dynamic.

Essential to the opening is a clearly projected and shapely melody with a gentle, legato accompaniment. A finger substitution of 2-1 on the LH's chord in bar 2 will help join the top notes, giving a nice smooth transition; this is particularly important when repeated in the *p* second phrase. Balance will be challenging in bars 17–20. Exaggerating the strong LH with softer RH in practice will help in developing control and therefore the ability to adjust from piano to piano. The articulation of the cuckoo call can be achieved in two ways: a strong bounce at the wrist onto the fingertips for the *f*, and subtle control with the finger from the surface of the key for the *p*.

There is no more imaginative way to inspire a confident shaping to the melody than to add words encouraging a characterful rise and fall in the dynamic throughout the phrases. Your student should make sure that the LH lifts its chord before the RH's final note (F), waiting just a fraction before the final call to enhance the cuckoo's last, cheeky entrance.

B:4 Gurlitt Jagdstückchen (Hunting)

The theme of hunting pervades children's piano pieces of the twentieth century. German hunting calls are all based around the harmonic series, which gives the characteristic intervals of this piece's opening bars. The ⁶₈ feel has the added bonus of implying a galloping horse.

The trickiest section is the final four bars which present challenges in hand coordination. Slow practice is essential, not just of the notes but of the phrasing too – deliberately releasing the RH's G in bar 21 but not the LH B♭, for instance. A decisive sense of pulse conveys the excitement of the chase, and, for hesitation to be avoided, rhythmic work is needed, and preparation of the phrase to follow. This is particularly relevant to the final chords: quick shadowing of these in the quaver rests will inspire confidence.

These hunting calls are to resound. They rely on projection, articulation and rhythm, enshrined in the marcato marking of the opening. Good clarity of tone with a direct, fingertip approach to the keys will give crispness and control. The horn notes can also be slurred, hence the phrasing in bar 3 which encourages a more shapely and overlapped sense of phrase. Vivid dynamic contrasts and good balance will bring the scene to life, and a steady but strongly insistent pulse will encapsulate the determination of the huntsmen.

B:5　Maconchy Sad Story

This meltingly sad piece would benefit from an appropriately sorrowful personal experience to inspire the mood. The RH melody is part song, part heartfelt sigh of a child, and conveys a strong melancholy, while the LH has a supportive role, its line interspersed with, perhaps, the soothing comments of a loving parent.

To encourage melodic projection and shape there needs to be a gradual release and support of weight behind the RH, and keeping hands close to the keys will help avoid an unwanted accent on the first note of a phrase as well as encourage a delicate tapering at the end. The warm accompanying chords need a pliant wrist and 'soft' fingers, releasing slowly into the bed of the keys.

The melody, almost throughout, asks for a beautifully blended legato, coupled with subtle dynamic shading within the phrases. The staccatos on the repeated Ds should not be too short (think of them as delicately sobbing), and while the dynamic contrasts suggest a growing anguish, care should be taken not to overdo this. In bar 19 the balance changes briefly to the LH, the RH having to stay softly out of the way while the LH reassuringly repeats the opening phrase. A sensitively judged ritardando will beautifully round off the sad scene.

B:6　Trad. Welsh David of the White Rock

The composer of this haunting and melancholy tune was the eighteenth-century harpist David Owen, who lived at a farm called 'The White Rock'. The Welsh words, added later by the poet John Hughes, tell the story of David wishing to play one final tune on the harp before he dies.

The sad tale is, in part, conveyed by the minor key. Practising both D minor and its relative F major should quickly familiarize the fingers with the physical feel of the scalic and arpeggio figures. The story will be best communicated by a persuasive balance between hands and a bold vocal musical shape to the tune. This is partly physical but having a vivid aural awareness and expectation of the sound will also help. Playing the piece as a duet with your student can nurture this, focusing on the balance between the hands and creating a discernible shape in the RH.

An appropriate relaxed tempo is significant and must be decided before the fingers play a note. Singing the final bars in the head with a slowing at the end, and then linking in the first two bars (as if starting a second verse), will encourage a more flexible and reflective opening. The relatively few dynamic markings provide a wonderful opportunity for students to add their own musical ideas to the words – an almost blank canvas to tell a poignant tale.

C:1 **Rob Hall** Asian Tiger Prowl

Tigers are among the most beautiful of wild animals. They like to live in rainforests where their handsome striped coats act like a camouflage. In this exciting piece one can imagine the tiger's stealthy movements as he creeps through the undergrowth. Tigers usually hunt alone and at the moment of striking can leap up to nine metres to grab their prey!

The composer's articulation marks are very precise; every tenuto line, accent and staccato dot must be meticulously observed. If your student has difficulty with the different types of touch, it will help to drop the hand into the tenuto notes while moving upwards when playing staccato notes. The syncopated rhythms in bars 11, 16 and 19 may prove tricky at first and require extra attention, and the important rests must be counted carefully – they seem to describe moments when the tiger pauses to watch. Maybe the hunted animal hears something rustling and looks around fearfully before resuming its grazing.

The 'stalking' figure of bars 1–2 returns in bar 12 an octave lower and louder only to be followed by a whole bar rest, a diminuendo and two quieter bars. The tiger is crouching, getting ready to pounce. A sudden rush and he leaps to make the kill! Pedal is essential here and should be depressed just after striking the penultimate chord and held through to the very end.

C:2 **Khachaturian** Skipping Rope

The need to compose 'music for the people' during the Soviet period has left us with a rich resource of teaching material. The Armenian composer Khachaturian was one of the most respected of Soviet composers, and like many of his colleagues he wrote his share of piano music for children.

This delightful description of children at play provides a great opportunity to hone staccato skills. A bright, crisp attack will be needed and attention given to the balance of the hands. The LH plays a supporting role throughout and should be a little quieter than the RH's melody. However, from bar 9 the accompaniment becomes legato and the descending chromatic notes will need to be heard as a countermelody. It will sound more effective and simpler in the long run if this melody is all legato rather than played with tiny breaks at each bar-line. The technique of managing different touches at the same time is a challenge that has to be tackled at some stage. For the sake of consistency, the melody upbeat A in bar 16 could be played by the RH.

The metronome tempo of ♩ = 144 and the given dynamic markings are sufficient to create the cheerful activity of this scene. Encourage your student to listen closely as the tied D at the end dies away so that the *rit.* and diminuendo can be perfectly judged.

C:3 Trad. American When the saints go marching in   (MMM)

This famous old American gospel hymn may not be so well known to younger generations, although it has been adopted as a rallying song by several football and rugby clubs in England and Australia. It is a popular number with jazz bands, and in this arrangement, with its swinging rhythms, the atmosphere of 1920s New Orleans can be imagined.

After a brief introduction, the simple melody begins in the LH before passing over to the RH in bar 12. There is little in the melody to tax your student; the challenge lies with the decorative, swinging figures. These will need to be practised slowly with a steady beat tapped out with the other hand. Encourage your student to do this at home so that practice between lessons is accurate. Most of the suggested fingering lies comfortably in the hands, but a less complicated version could be tried for the first three bars: in the RH finger 3 might be used on F and finger 4 on F♯, and in the LH finger 4 on E, finger 3 on F and finger 2 on F♯.

Once it is thoroughly secure, the piece can begin to move towards a brisk marching tempo, felt as two-in-a-bar rather than four. Dynamics should be positive and varied, and the accents firmly marked in order to convey the energy and spirit of the music.

C:4 Paul Drayton Chatterbox Charlie   (MMM)

Originating in Trinidad and Tobago, calypso very quickly spread across the world. With infectious rhythms and jaunty lyrics it is full of good humour, and immediately sets the toes tapping. In 'Chatterbox Charlie' one can imagine the non-stop comments and questions of a precocious youngster.

In performance it needs crisp staccato, marked accents and a firm beat throughout. The piece makes an excellent study for the development of staccato touches as almost every quaver is staccato. Only those notes with ties, slurs or accents will need to be held. A light arm staccato is the simplest technique for most of the notes, changing to hand (wrist) staccato for the 3rds and 5ths in bars 9, 11 and 13. The tempo is not unduly fast. A speed of ♩ = *c*.120 will bring the piece to life as long as the articulation is neat and the dynamics observed.

Although the phrasing has a regular four-bar shape, it is best to forget the bar-lines and allow each group of quavers to lead to the accented notes. This will help to highlight the syncopated character of the music. Warn your student to count carefully at the last bar – there is a danger of beginning the LH quavers late. A ritenuto is not needed at the end, although some might like a slight delay for the final chord.

C:5 Eben The Huntsman and the Maidens (MMM)

Following in the footsteps of Béla Bartók, the Czech composer Petr Eben arranged many of his own national folk tunes for young pianists. The story behind this piece is not dissimilar to Cinderella – a king out hunting, a lovely young girl made to stay home and do the work, a cruel mother and sister. The plot is rather more grisly than Cinderella's, but it has inspired a number of works, including Dvořák's tone poem *The Golden Spinning Wheel*.

Before practice begins, a decision must be made about fingering – whether to change fingers for repeated notes or simply use the same finger. If the former, a consistent fingering should be found, like 4-3-2-1 for the quavers in bars 1 and 5 and then 2-1-4 for the figure in bars 2 and 6. However, a tempo of ♩ = *c*.100 would not be fast, and as long as your student lets the arm bounce loosely on the staccato notes, it is less complicated to use the same finger. The main challenge for the pianist is managing staccato in one hand while the other plays legato, so careful separate-hands practice and listening should be encouraged.

The mood is cheerful, the staccato quavers suggesting the trotting of the horse as the king rides out to meet the maidens. It ends with a flourish, and pedal could be used to connect the last two chords.

C:6 Simone Plé La petite troupe (The Little Troop) (MMM)

The marching tempo and trumpet-like melodies of this lively piece conjure up the image of tin soldiers on parade. At the very outset it is important to notice the phrase structure so that the music can flow naturally.

It begins with a simple four-bar phrase which is answered by a five-bar phrase. This pattern continues until two phrases of four bars at the end. There are just two tunes, repeated in different parts of the keyboard with a LH accompaniment that sounds like a drumbeat. Crisp staccato will be needed together with a strict pulse. A tempo of ♩ = *c*.120 will convey the steady marching of the troop. By showing your student in advance how most of the notes of the RH melody fit within the C major tonic triad wherever they are on the keyboard, worries about all those leger lines can be avoided!

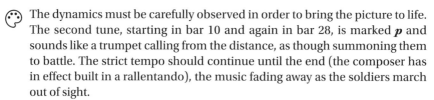 The dynamics must be carefully observed in order to bring the picture to life. The second tune, starting in bar 10 and again in bar 28, is marked *p* and sounds like a trumpet calling from the distance, as though summoning them to battle. The strict tempo should continue until the end (the composer has in effect built in a rallentando), the music fading away as the soldiers march out of sight.

GRADE 2

A:1 **Attwood** Allegretto (MMM)

Thomas Attwood's career as a composer was both distinguished and long. He studied in Vienna with Mozart, who thought very highly of him. In 1796 he became both organist of St Paul's Cathedral in London, and composer of the Chapel Royal, writing music for George IV and William IV. At the time of his death he was preparing an anthem for the coronation of Queen Victoria.

Attwood's keyboard music is clearly influenced by Mozart, as can be heard in this charming Allegretto. The four-bar phrases all have a natural rise and fall, sometimes peaking at the second bar (bars 2 and 6) or in the third (bars 11 and 15). A warm cantabile tone will be required. The accompaniment is best practised in block chords at first. This will help your student to recognize chords at a glance and to make the octave shift at bar 5 more confidently. The fourth finger may be preferred for the bass note of the chord in bar 1, reserving the fifth for E in bar 3. Holding down the lowest notes (finger-pedalling) will add warmth to the texture.

Although this piece works perfectly well without the sustaining pedal, those who are able might like to add it to bars 9–10 and bars 13–14, changing with each new harmony. This brings a contrasting colour to the middle section.

A:2 **Mozart** Ein Mädchen oder Weibchen (For a Girl or a Woman) (MMM)

Mozart's opera *The Magic Flute* was premiered in Vienna less than three months before his untimely death in December 1791. It was a huge success and has remained immensely popular ever since. This aria is sung by the bird-catcher, Papageno, and tells of his longing to find a wife. As he sings he accompanies himself on the magic bells he has been given as a talisman.

It will be important to keep the staccato and various rhythms really crisp. The dotted-note figures seen in several bars must not be allowed to slacken into triplets, and in bar 6 there might be a temptation to delay the start of the tinkling semiquavers. In order to avoid the RH having to move forwards to place the thumb on a black note, your student might prefer to try the following fingering in bar 1: keep the third finger on D and play the E/C♯ with 4/2, changing to second finger for the last beat. The LH plays the role of accompanist throughout and must always be a little quieter than the melody.

Performances of this aria are readily available online, and seeing Papageno dressed in his bird-like costume will help your student to understand the rather whimsical character of the music.

A:3 | Susato La Mourisque

Tylman Susato lived and worked in Antwerp during the sixteenth century. He wrote many instrumental pieces and as a publisher did his best to promote Flemish music. *La Mourisque* is a Moorish dance, often described as a basse dance, and some believe it to be related to the English Morris dance.

There is a danger that the performance will sound too square. The suggested metronome speed of ♩ = *c.*72 gives a clue as to its rhythmic impetus. It must be felt as two-in-a-bar, not four, and in the first and third sections the stress falls at the beginning of every second bar. In the quieter middle section stresses occur only on the fourth and eighth bars. By avoiding too many first-beat accents, the music will come to life. Dynamic markings provide plenty of variety, and if observed, slurs and staccato notes will give a pleasing lilt. If your student's hand cannot manage the octaves in bars 17, 21 and 25 comfortably, the top note may be omitted (as shown in the score).

The dance is stately in character, and one can imagine it being played by trumpets, drums and tambourine (Susato was a trumpet player in the town band). Rather than slowing down towards the end, your student might delay the final chord a little to indicate the dancers bowing to each other.

A:4 | Jeremiah Clarke The Prince of Denmark's March

D major is often used for martial or ceremonial music and with this famous melody one can imagine the pomp and colour of a royal occasion as the trumpets herald the arrival of the monarch.

Two main issues have to be settled before any serious practice can begin – articulation and fingering. A simple solution is to play all the crotchets staccato, but this denies the piece expression and buoyancy. There is no definitive answer, but one interpretation of the rondo theme might be to play the melody largely legato, but to make natural breaks just before each of the ornaments.

In bar 4 a slur from first to second beat followed by staccato notes will give shape to the end of the first phrase. In bars 2 and 6 the third- and fourth-beat crotchets will sound effective if they, too, are staccato, and a slur from the first to the second beat of bar 7 announces the cadence. Meanwhile the LH has some two-part challenges. In bar 1 (and similar) the minims must be held while the crotchets are played staccato; students shouldn't be afraid to use the thumb on consecutive notes if necessary.

There are no dynamic marks in the recommended edition, so your student should be encouraged to devise a plan. There is scope for echo effects and terraced dynamics, but tradition tells us it should begin and end loudly.

A:5 **L. Mozart** Polonaise in C

The Polonaise is a stately processional dance in triple time. The dancers walk round the ballroom with a dipping movement on every third beat. This movement and stress on the last beat of the bar can be seen in a beautiful demonstration of the dance on a website called *The Polish Zone*, which is well worth a look.

With the character of the dance in mind, a tempo of ♩ = *c.*63 will be comfortable. The RH melody is gracefully shaped with slurs that provide a pleasing lilt, and the gliding movement of the dancers on third beats will be well portrayed if the crotchets are held for full value. The stately movement of the crotchets in the LH melody is best expressed with a legato touch, but the quavers inject more movement and sound effective if they are played staccato.

The dynamic marks given in the recommended edition work well, but there should also be nuances within each dynamic level to give shape to phrasing. For instance, after the bold start a slight diminuendo might be made towards the end of bar 2. A little crescendo in bar 3 then leads to the highest point of the first complete phrase, and so on. By marking firmly the three chords of the penultimate bar and slightly delaying the very last note the dance will end with a flourish.

A:6 **Telemann** Dolce

The gentle, melancholy mood of this beautiful piece will appeal to the more thoughtful student. As with many pieces in ⅜ time, it should be felt as one-in-a-bar. Once the notes are known, a tempo of ♩. = *c.*42 will give it sufficient momentum while allowing time for expression. Accents on every first beat should be avoided at all costs.

It takes the form of a simple duet, each part as important as the other. Your student might like to imagine the colour of instruments like oboe and bassoon while playing. This image would also help with the idea of taking tiny breaths between phrases or at sudden changes of dynamic. This is done by slightly shortening the last note of a phrase, as in bar 8, not delaying the start of the next. The touch should be legato, but with a few detached notes following slurs and at the approach to cadences (quavers 2 and 3 in bar 7, for instance).

The music contains a variety of moods as it passes through different keys: B minor to D major, then E minor through A major and back to B minor. The second theme (beginning on the upbeat into bar 17), with its modulations and semitone steps, has an altogether darker colouring. This is a piece to cherish!

B:1 Reinecke Song

Your student might enjoy composing words that fit the gentle, sweet mood of this song, especially if they can reflect the melodically beautiful rising 7ths which taper away afterwards. Although the piece looks rather unchanging on the page, a search among its wide-reaching intervals and telling modulations could inspire meaningful words and, in turn, a sense of ownership of the song's emotional effect.

The first technical challenge is to produce a sufficiently singing tone in the RH. A pliably firm finger touch, supported by supple wrists, facilitates clear projection and a smoothly shaped line. The accompanying LH quavers need to be as inconspicuous as possible. Keeping the finger movements small, barely raising the keys to their resting level, will help here. Slightly sustaining the bass outline (below the thumb quavers), to give a little tonal smudging, can add warmth within a murmuring texture, but might require considerable LH practice.

The music's most expressive performances will find scope for flexible rhythmic flow, allowing phrase endings to settle and breathe. Taking even a little longer in the middle of bars 4, 8 and 14 gives a sense of repose and helps convey the overall shape well. The 'magic moment' is in bars 18–20; giving extra energy to this unexpectedly long phrase prepares for the radiantly hovering B♭ in bar 20 and the peaceful close.

B:2 Smetana Waltz in G

Pianists who enjoy acting the clown will relish this perky little number. Major chords and rhythmic momentum create perpetual high spirits; even the brief modulation to the minor has a quality of crocodile tears, so quickly does the good cheer return.

Technically, there are no special problems, apart from the rather active LH in bars 14–15. A small ritardando here could underline the change to minor and ease note-finding; picking up the RH with eagerness in bar 16 will regain the music's forward drive. Overall, balance between the hands needs care, especially at the start; the melody should sing out clearly, so the LH might reduce the accompaniment level almost to *p*. Although slow practice will initially help ensure accuracy and, in the last line, communication of the detail, a brisk tempo is ultimately desirable.

Gradually building to a boisterous finish, the performance will benefit from a sense of dance. Lightening the second and third LH crotchets in each bar, where they are double notes, will give a waltz feel. Overall, the simple phrase structure needs less weight on every second bar – hence the start of bars 1, 3 and 5 will be stronger than the intervening crotchets. A final touch of panache can highlight the colourful harmony of bar 30, slightly holding the tempo back for emphasis, prior to the comically insistent end.

B:3 S. Wilson The Stowaway

An intriguing mix of sea-shanty melody with the markings to play quietly, stealthily, captures the title's image perfectly. The athletic LH, at unusually low pitch, and the robust dancing rhythms will encourage agility in weak fingers, while making the fingers' owners proud of the impressive musical result.

The nippy tempo requires secure fingering patterns, to avoid trips in performance. The last LH crotchets of bars 10 and 14 are especially treacherous, as they may become confused and lead to error in the following bars. A pleasing melodic line is created at the top of the descending RH chords of bars 5–7. Here, an ability to lean slightly into the outer side of the RH, while keeping the chord notes striking simultaneously, will allow their melody to ring out. The more joined-up these chords can be, the better; fingers should cling on until absolutely needed for the next chord.

Refined tonal control in pedalled minim bars can add polish. The use of the pedal may be a new pleasure at Grade 2 and could require a different sitting position from normal. Listening to a few real sea shanties could help inspire your student in bringing the character to life. Irresistible rhythmic vitality, achieved by lightening second and fourth beats, might especially enhance the bouncy middle section.

B:4 Bortkiewicz Through the Desert

This unusual piece will intrigue students with its image of a 'caravan' of camels and loose-robed traders traversing the hot sand. Perhaps the caravan is in two slightly separated groups, because the piece is notable for the strict canon between the hands, almost as if the song is delayed before the second group commences.

Although the piece has no obvious technical difficulties, there are a few pointers to remember, in order to create good balance between the hands and an expressive singing shape. The first is to begin each phrase smoothly, without accenting the opening upbeat notes or any note which follows a tie. This might be practised by playing both hands in unison, starting together and reading from either treble or bass clef. All dynamic details should be explored, to give musical shape to the phrases. The grace notes towards the end can be performed as two light demisemiquavers taken out of the previous C quaver, with the ensuing B quaver given slight extra weight.

The final stage of putting the canon together correctly should give much delight and no small challenge! Each hand takes over the limelight as the previous hand's phrase reaches its restful conclusion. Highest marks will be achieved by players who can master this sense of conversation, with the phrasing's rise and fall expressed through smooth legato and good dynamic control.

B:5 Gedike Petite Pièce

The title offers little to help convey an image of what occurs within. Performers might like to imagine a small bird or butterfly passing, with the more surprising harmonies perhaps indicating a glimpse of warm sunshine, or a fleeting chill in the air. The music's delicacy would suit small hands; lightness of touch is an advantage, provided that more robust tone can be achieved where requested.

The sighing shapes, as in bars 2 and 4, should be phrased off gently. Further expressive touches occur in bars 5–8. There, the RH melody is balanced by an equally lovely one at the top of the LH, which needs to project a little in order to sing out. The strong chord in bar 23 needs forearm weight without allowing the fingers to collapse underneath. The points of pedal here and in bar 25 give no difficulty, but add greatly to the beauty of sound.

As notes become more familiar, a graceful feel can be acquired by developing subtly flowing movements in the wrists, sinking into the keys as semiquaver bars start and lifting as they finish staccato. When the imagined creature flies up and away near the end, the long silences should be carefully counted through in quavers (as also the sustained chords earlier), so that subsequent notes are placed with no sense of rush.

B:6 Holst Jupiter

As well as starring in Holst's popular orchestral suite *The Planets*, this melody features in a much-loved hymn, so it conveys meaning to many people. Singing tone and expressive phrasing will be the keys to a good performance.

The directions of cantabile and maestoso need the RH fingertips to play firmly into the keys, with hand weight supported by the wrist to avoid heavy accents. Dynamic shading can enhance the tune's rise and fall, with phrase endings finding a momentary sense of repose. At the final *rall.*, pedal used on upbeat crotchets and the final chord could add grandeur, as long as care is taken not to smudge the changes of harmony.

The most successful accounts of this piece will give it a sense of direction and balance between the hands. Precise placing of rests in bars 1–6 (and 17–22) can encourage a purposeful momentum across bar-lines, propelling the music forwards. Where LH second beats are not silent, an opportunity arises to create an even longer sense of line in the phrasing. In these phrases of the middle section, the LH might project more as duet partner and help to build richer tone towards the final climax. While practising to achieve these qualities, your student might enjoy composing words to sing during the music. Any heartfelt thoughts will suffice, provided that the lines match the musical phrasing.

[C:1] **Trad. Scottish** The Piper o' Dundee

Imagining bagpipers clad in tartan kilts, surrounded by lochs and heather, will help your students be immersed in this vibrant number. Richard Michael cleverly continues the century-old tradition of adding Scots songs to modern melodies; he is a great jazz-educationalist, passionately committed to swinging open the jazz doors to more players.

The daring mix of traditional Scots music with a jazz groove will require the performer to commit to the sudden changes of dynamics and articulation. The staccato upbeat can be used to land on the downbeat, helping to highlight the opening line-voicing and create rhythmic energy. Not to be missed is the clever quote of 'Auld Lang Syne' woven into the melody from bar 8, followed by the swift crescendo leading towards the pause at bar 14. The sudden accents will reinforce those strong, characteristic first and third beats – and the chord shapes need to be rigorously well-prepared to alleviate unwanted pauses over changes of hand position. The LH drone effect at bar 17 needs to be well coordinated with the return of the opening melody, now developed.

The imitative entries throughout the piece need to be approached with a sense of fun to achieve the specific articulation and embrace the style of the piece. The control of the *rit.* and crescendo might present a challenge but exploring how quickly the crescendo can be made will inspire.

[C:2] **Prokofiev** The Cat

Peter and the Wolf, one of Prokofiev's most famous works, was composed in 1936 amid political turmoil. Prokofiev had just returned to Moscow after touring Europe and the USA, keen to build bridges with his homeland. He trod a fine line in his compositions between appeasing Stalin and writing freely. Natalia Satz, from the Central Children's Theatre in Moscow, commissioned him to write a 'symphonic fairy tale ... accompanied by narration.' Prokofiev wrote the story himself and composed the work in a week.

The pictorial imagery of this light-footed cat stealthily hunting the bird is expressed using low-range staccato notes, played in the original orchestral version on the clarinet. Encourage experimentation of staccato lengths and touches to mimic the cat's steps around the garden. Attention will need to be given to the changes of stave and of hand position as the piece modulates. Listening to a recording of the piece should enthuse the most reluctant of pianists to explore the slurs, heavy tenutos and orchestral textures.

Grading the dynamics as the register gets higher will add to the tension and, during the lesson, accompanying your student's playing with the narration will reinforce a sense of performance. Ideally, a flexible rubato in the cat leitmotif will heighten the feeling of anticipation in the melody. The clever cat will get its reward for hard work on articulation!

C:3 **Schmitz** Gospel Flair

The *Mini Jazz* series, from which this piece comes, is in effect a cumulative study of jazz rhythms and licks, used for building up and extending basic hand positions. The use of different accents establishes the feel of each piece; *Gospel Flair* characterizes gospel with its heavy offbeat rhythms, 'blue' notes and call-and-answer phrases with RH solos followed by 'Amen' chord responses.

The tempo will have to be built up slowly with the metronome so that rhythmic energy is always there, even in the rests. The unisons need to be linked in, as if they are jazz solos, with the band interjecting on the chords. Taking time over the accuracy of the fingering, accents and staccatos will help to maintain the drive. The quick jumps between staves can be practised by arriving at the chord before needing to play it; making this a lively game will encourage your students to achieve the passages correctly.

Making sure that the heavy accents are communicated effectively will help to lock into the jazz style. Playing with a non-classical, deep touch into the keys, with an almost percussive hitting of the keys, will help to create a stylish performance and a convincing jazz tone. As Schmitz himself wrote, players can 'have lots of fun'. Students should aim to show the piano at its best as part of the percussion family.

C:4 **Eben** The Goose-girl in Winter

Eben's (1929–2007) compositions uniquely combine rural Czech influence with that of his horrific experiences in a German World War II concentration camp. The piquant harmonies in the LH are characteristic of his style, but the music's programmatic and pedagogical nature shows his commitment to children's music-making. Perhaps inspired by the Brothers Grimm folk story entitled *The Goose Girl*, the staccato melodies reflect the icy conditions as the girl tiptoes feeding the geese.

Creative students will enjoy the contrasting articulation in the staccato melody leading to the tenuto at the second bar. Managing wrist weight on the tenuto will require work, as will coordinating the transfer of melody between the hands: practising scales with one hand staccato and the other legato will help here. The hand crossings at bar 18, which are exciting but difficult, need to be played with great ease and shape of phrase. A game of jumping the RH across the LH from one C to the C two octaves lower will ensure control.

Maintaining a natural sense of pulse while achieving the pianistic acrobatics will be the main challenge in this piece, and coming up with different articulation and balance games will inspire the less coordinated student. Once the definition in contrast and touch is achieved, the final *ritard.* needs to be observed to bring the piece to a satisfying close.

C:5 Simone Plé La poule dans le jardin (The Hen in the Garden)

Aged 21 when the iconic Debussy died, Plé taught at the Paris Conservatoire as a specialist in fugue composition and counterpoint. She lived through two world wars and saw the changing face of France. Taken from *Les Chants et les jeux* (1929), a set of 20 short pedagogical piano pieces, this witty piece portrays country life combined with late-French Impressionism.

The imaginative pianist will enjoy lifting the fingers quickly in imitation of the hen's head darting to the ground, pecking away at the seed. Meticulous LH-only practice will help with controlling the staccato, and a metronome will help in achieving a regular tempo. Make sure the RH prevails, differentiating between staccato and well-held tenuto. The change of position in the RH needs attention at bar 14, where rising 3rds in both hands move over the black notes.

The programmatic representation of the hen, clucking this way and that around the garden, dominates the piece. A performance will come alive if the sudden changes of dynamic from loud to quiet and the articulation contrasts are successfully achieved. In fact, the silences are as important as the notes in capturing the rhythmic crispness and vibrancy of attack. A strong sense of pulse is needed and counting the rests is imperative. Once the pulse is established, the subsequent tempo changes from bar 21 will be all the more effective.

C:6 Sarah Watts Rock Pools

An inventive and instinctive educationalist, Sarah Watts has created an impressive library of teaching pieces in the rock and jazz style. The characteristic 'Rock feel' indication invites the player into the world of rock with its infectious beat and memorable rhythms. The driving bass line combined with the RH solos are what gives the piece both its energy and groove.

A strong hand shape is needed from the start to achieve good voicing and confident chord patterns. Playing to the bottom of the key in a non-classical style will really reinforce stylistic understanding. Make sure that students take heed of the slurred 3rds; chord accuracy will be heightened by awareness of the fingering and pattern shapes. Throughout, the silences are as effective as the notes. Instilling a good sense of pulse, underpinned through metronome practice, will produce dividends in achieving stylistic success.

Delivering a strong rock feel with toe-tapping accuracy is essential while maintaining a good eye for the varying articulation and block dynamics. Practice involving rhythmic subdivision will lock down the quaver beats and rhythms and so help internalize the feel. The RH solos (e.g. bars 7–8) need great confidence with a heavy, rhythmic touch; this heavier tone might therefore suit the pianist whose tone at this stage is less well-rounded.

GRADE 3

A:1 | **Handel** Sonatina in G

This delightful contrapuntal piece is short, but it has plenty to say. An animated conversation takes place throughout between the two parts, which both make a strong statement at the start. The music should sound busy and purposeful but never hurried; you and your student will need to select a tempo at which the piece can flow with momentum and direction, but with all the notes articulated cleanly and evenly.

Fluent fingerwork is paramount in this piece – the running quavers should be legato but clearly articulated and with no hint of overlapping notes. Slow practice will be beneficial, perhaps using dotted rhythms while working at particular sequences. Fingering is a matter of individual preference, but the best selections will avoid awkward stretches and enable a comfortable hand shape to be maintained, particularly in passages such as bars 3–4 (RH) and 14–16 (LH).

Treating each part as an independent voice within this style is a good starting point. Sometimes one or other will dominate slightly, but working out the rise and fall within phrases in each voice will help define the expressive character. Dynamics are for individual choice but there should be plenty of light and shade, as in any dialogue. Emphasizing the upper note of the octave jumps in bars 1, 2 and 8 will give a strong rhythmic impulse to the music, and a slight slowing at the end could help to round it off decisively.

A:2 | **Mozart** Romanze

This sublimely beautiful piece, an arrangement of one of Mozart's most famous instrumental works, combines profound expression and tenderness with simplicity and economy in the writing. The heartfelt, delicate *Romanze* is also dignified and elegant, offering students a good opportunity to communicate effectively while having relatively few notes to play. It should flow with movement and direction, but with enough time and space to make every note count; nothing is superfluous.

The notes are easily assimilated; the challenge here is about creating mood and cantabile sound. A smooth legato touch, deep into the keys, will need fingerings to facilitate it. Students might prefer 2-1-4-3 for the semiquavers in bars 8 and 10, but 2-3-5-4 is an alternative. Staccatos should be gracefully lifted, not too clipped, with the melody projecting over the accompaniment throughout. Singing the phrases to understand their shape before playing them on the keyboard would be a useful exercise.

Some dynamics are already in the score, but a truly expressive performance will contain more. For example, the first full bar builds gradually before a diminuendo on the first beat of the next. The second note of the slurred quavers is lighter and shorter than the first, and the pace eases just a little at the *poco rit.* in bar 12. Listening to the original string version will help your student to appreciate the effortless cantabile and delicate textures so typical of Mozart.

[A:3] Beethoven German Dance in B flat (NO)

A robust conversation takes place between the hands in the outer sections of this sprightly and vigorous dance, the neat flicks of the grace notes adding character and rhythmic vitality. The Trio flows more smoothly with elegance in its well-mannered descending sequences and cadences before the return of the more rumbustious opening. The tempo need not be too quick but with enough momentum to flow at one-in-a-bar.

Nothing is particularly fast-moving here, but firm fingers are needed to grasp the chords securely, with a flick of the wrist off the first of the repeated chords. The wrist can also be involved in the grace notes, a little clockwise rotation coupled with positive articulation helping to make the two notes sound clean and distinct. Your students could practise voicing the top notes of the chords by leaning a little more weight into them – a very valuable skill to acquire.

Varied articulation will form a major part of a characterful performance. A firm first note on each slur, followed by a lighter, shorter second note, lifted upbeats, crisp attack on the sforzandos, and a slightly accented staccato on the third beats in bars 5–7 and 13–15 will give the outer sections personality and vigour, all within a context of strong but never strident tone. Smooth legato playing of the slurred notes and detached but not overly short crotchet chords should give the Trio a gentler feel, coupled with a softer dynamic.

[A:4] J. S. Bach Bourrée (NO)

This lively, outgoing dance has a straightforwardly cheerful air and should flow briskly with a feeling of two-in-a-bar. Bach takes us for a bracing and invigorating jog, briefly visiting some neighbouring keys before heading purposefully home to F major at the main cadences. There are plenty of notes to master, but the reprise from bar 17 to the end means that there is less to learn than first appears!

Sprightly and precise finger action will be needed, with numerous fingering options to consider. The music can be divided into four-bar sections for ease of practising; this is also useful when building up to performance tempo (keeping the pulse stable throughout). There need not be much difference in the balance between the parts but it is important that the bass doesn't dominate.

The music does not need big contrasts in dynamics, but you can help your student to identify the natural shapes within two- and four-bar sections and to realize them with subtle rise and fall in the sound. The tone should be bright and clear with *mf* a good basic volume to start from. The articulation might be predominantly smooth or detached, or a combination of both, as long as the approach is consistent. The repeated crotchets in bars 2, 6, 18 and 22 lend themselves to being lifted, and the main sections rounded off with a slight diminuendo in the ascending LH notes.

A:5   **Mozart**   Menuett in F

This Menuett is a characterful and graceful dance. Mozart alternates a step-like melody, sometimes off the beat, with precise repeated notes and purposeful sprints towards the cadences. Imagining the two hands as dance partners might be fun – sometimes they move as equals but at others the man anchors the pair to the floor while the lady displays her agility! Fingerwork needs to be positive and firm throughout.

Choice of tempo is critical, best judged by the pace at which the semiquavers can be fluently played while maintaining the pulse. This is most easily achieved with a 5-3-2-1 fingering on each set, although 4-2-1-2 for the third beat of bars 19 and 21 may be preferred. The balance should generally be weighted to slightly favour the RH part, but equal sound from treble and bass will suit the conversational opening bars.

Variation in tone and articulation will be key to establishing the musical character. The repeated notes will benefit from a really crisp bounce, although slurring the octave jumps, by stretch or a dab of pedal, provides a touch of elegance. The LH's continuous quavers could be slightly detached, while firmly joined crotchets would successfully underpin the semiquavers. The more shapely bars 11–14 perhaps call for a smoother touch, adding to the expressive range. Wide dynamic contrasts, graded rise and fall within the phrases (sometimes over two bars, sometimes four), and a slight diminuendo in bars 10 and 22 complete the musical picture.

A:6   **Trad. English**   Staines Morris

This music has a long history. Originally an Elizabethan lute piece, it was subsequently married to the text of the 'Maypole Song', dating from the Restoration, which exhorts young men to bring their ladies to dance and celebrate the spring. After a courtly opening bow the music moves through a series of two-bar phrases in the style of a formal dance, laced with some delightful chromatic bass notes. After another bow a reflective final line recalls the fun, and fades with a weary but contented smile in the tonic major.

The notes are straightforward, although precise and smooth fingerwork will be needed for the legato RH chords in bars 21–2 and for the last three bars where the LH splits into two voices. Using the pedal will create attractive sonority in the open 5ths, changing it perhaps on the first beats of bars 3 and 31.

Shapely rise and fall in the tone within each phrase will give the music character, but encourage your student to vary the amounts, maintaining interest. The repeated notes in bars 13 and 17 suggest a more energetic mood, as does the relative major tonality – and a more detached touch on those would convey this. The details should be savoured: the expressive chromaticism, the softer sound of the closing bow, and the slowing at the end as sleep beckons. The final notes can linger until the sound is almost completely gone.

[B:1] Dibdin Tom Bowling (TB)

Sadness and pathos pervade this song of mourning with its undulating phrases and gentle rhythmic flow. Notes generally lie easily under the fingers, with no large stretches, and the sustained harmonies provide the perfect opportunity to introduce legato pedalling. Singing the melody at a comfortable pitch, breathing where indicated by the phrase marks, will allow your student to understand both the length and shape of phrases.

The ear is the best guide to achieving perfect legato, without any overlap of the fingers, while practising the melody and bass lines of the outer sections, silently 'shadowing' the inner notes, will provide the physical sensation of the different levels of weight needed for effective balance. Although the opening bars are reliant on the pedal (changed twice per bar) to sustain the harmonies, your student may prefer to use a finger legato for the bars with more frequent harmonic changes.

Each of the four melodic phrases, which span either four or six bars, has a natural ebb and flow. The warmth of the human voice can be emulated in the cantabile melody, and sensitively judged rubato, balancing any forward impetus with slight slackening of pace, will breathe life into the musical line. The focal point provided by the *largamente* at bar 10 and the C♮ at bar 13 are special moments not to be overlooked, while the tenderness of the final bars seems to convey a sense of the spirit rising heavenwards.

[B:2] Hiller Polnisches Lied (Polish Song) (TB)

This piece, an excellent choice for developing musicality, seems to express both melancholy and patriotic pride. Its soulful melody appears three times in different guises, variation-like, the final statement giving the opportunity to explore a melodic line in bass register. The dance rhythms, often with a highlighted second beat, unfold gently, and switches in tonality between minor and major reflect the changes of mood.

Well-measured note lengths, giving full value to the crotchets, will convey the rhythmic poise of this graceful dance. Staccato semiquavers, slightly separated, contrast with smoother lines, and the LH dotted crotchets in the opening bars serve to sustain the third strand of the texture through the bar. Confident LH semiquavers will enable seamless rhythmic flow at bar 13, while coordination in the following bars may need some attention in order to achieve clarity in the overlapping phrasing.

The generous amount of musical detail on the page provides clues to inflection of phrases. Each *f* provides a richly sonorous highlight, with tenuto marks suggesting prominence on some second beats and well-managed key control allowing each hand to create its own independent shape. The LH line, always subservient to the main melody, gives greater intensity for the espressivo repeat at bar 13, while imagining the sonority of the bass voice or cello may help to project the bass line as the LH takes centre stage latterly, this time with the RH offering its own expressive contours.

B:3 Tchaikovsky Marche des soldats de bois (TB) (March of the Wooden Soldiers)

Tchaikovsky's *Album for the Young*, a treasure trove of pieces equal in stature to Schumann's collection of the same name, explores the world of childhood imagination. Here the treble register, a melodic range of less than an octave and the quiet dynamic level all contribute towards the miniature feel of this March. Although the regular eight-bar phrase structure suggests the discipline of military marching, accents seem to throw the natural shape of the phrase off balance as if mimicking the awkward movements of wooden joints.

Precise control, using the tips of the fingers and keeping in close contact with the keys, is needed to ensure all notes 'speak' in the *pp* sections. Equal agility in both hands will enable them to remain neatly synchronized, while consistency and sprightliness in the all-important dotted rhythms might be helped by imagining the semiquaver as a grace note preceding the following longer note. Experimentation will reveal the most effective fingering for the LH repeated note 'drum rolls' (e.g. at bar 8), a light touch enabling the key to rebound for true clarity.

Two distinct types of slur occur throughout. Accents, always within the context of the childlike mood, highlight the start of strong/weak slurs, whereas a gentle 'kick' off the second note of those beginning on a semiquaver will preserve normal emphasis. Your student can find a warmer sound for the slightly louder middle section, enjoying the harmonic colour provided by chords such as that in bar 18 along the way.

B:4 J. F. F. Burgmüller Angelic Harmony (TB)

An ethereal quality, as if from the skies, seems to permeate this beautiful piece with its swirling, gently flowing triplets and the harmonic progressions which suggest broad phrase shapes. An unhurried, yet fluid tempo seems to suit the mood, an effective performance dependent on even fingerwork with gentle, subtle inflections of tone.

Practising the triplets in block chords may help to secure the shapes under the fingers. Your student should aim for perfect equality as the figuration passes effortlessly between the hands, with no bump on thumb notes. A little lateral wrist movement aids facility around the keyboard, especially for the wider RH stretches, while helping to feature the fifth finger, which often provides a melodic line. Optional use of pedal, changing with each new harmony, enhances the *armonioso* character, although, equally, it is possible to sustain the harmonies with the fingers alone.

The structure consists of three main sections, followed by a coda. Gentle crescendos highlight the arching phrase shapes, and subtle use of rubato enhances the fluidity of the triplets. The shift to E minor at bar 9 seems to signal a more dramatic, urgent mood than elsewhere, especially at the tenor voice's entry at bar 13. Rests at ends of sections serve to let the air into an otherwise sustained harmonic texture, and the serenity of the *più lento* chords, sensitively balanced to highlight the top note, adds an almost prayer-like character to the ending.

B:5 Carroll Dwarfs of the Mist (TB)

Walter Carroll produced many attractive, descriptive pieces which fit comfortably under the hands of the developing player. If the introductory quote from Sir Walter Scott fails to resonate today, the instruction 'grotesque' probably will. Imagining a woodland scene, mistily spooky in the twilight, will be helpful, and there is vivid musical detail to create mystery and surprise.

Choosing a tempo which can be reliably maintained, saving a little speed for the accelerando and presto at the end, is vital for a successful performance. Limbering-up exercises, especially for fingers 3, 4 and 5, may help the semiquavers, which need equal agility and clarity in both hands. A firm pulse throughout, with ties given full value, highlights the alert, sprightly mood. Rests often serve to provide space for shifts of hand position. Pedalling, although optional, adds colour to harmonies at key points; however, a crisper unpedalled effect may be preferred for the ending.

Candidates often think they are making clear dynamic contrasts when, in fact, little is coming across – it is practically impossible to overdo them here! Springing off the end of the semiquaver figures draws attention to the main beats while accents and tenuto marks slightly displace the bar's natural stress.

Energy and impetus evaporate at bars 29–31, the piece's quietest point, before resuming for the final 'sprint'. Hand staccato facilitates agility and attack for the presto as it moves confidently towards the final chord, with the grace notes, placed before the beat, adding extra sparkle.

B:6 Saint-Saëns L'éléphant (The Elephant)

The deep register and deliberate rhythms of this piece, a double bass solo in the original chamber version, capture perfectly the slow-moving gait, cumbersome yet graceful, of this most endearing of animals. The humour in casting this in waltz style is further enhanced by the inclusion in bars 21–4 of a quote (some three octaves below the original) from the Ballet of Sylphs from Berlioz's *The Damnation of Faust*.

Although the LH provides the main melodic interest, the RH chords are likely to present the greater challenge. The final four bars, with their four distinct RH positions, may benefit from being memorized in order to manage the leaps accurately. A curved hand position will help ensure all chord notes sound together, and smooth transitions can be achieved by using the fourth finger for some top notes, as recommended.

Weighty chords, both of equal length, establish the plodding character of the four-bar introduction. Thereafter the RH plays a subservient role to its partner, whose accents and slurs provide a dance-like elegance, especially when second and third beats are lightened. Although not obligatory, detaching the quavers adds to the ponderous effect, in addition to evoking the separate bowstrokes of the original. Smoother, quieter lines at bar 21 add welcome relief before the somewhat abrupt ending. The temptation to hurry these final bars should be resisted and the contrast between slurs and staccato, with extra attack on the accents, can be enjoyed.

C:1 Kabalevsky Clowns

Immediately attractive contradictions of tonality set the comic scene of this circus-type tune. The composer's Violin Concerto, Op. 48 starts in similar mood and would make enjoyable listening before or during the learning of this tiny miniature. Rapid running notes, spiky accompaniment and witty nudges in the rhythm abound; it is easy to picture clowns with bicycles and buckets of water creating mayhem.

Finding evenness in the semiquavers may require some preliminary technical groundwork, although the notes are straightforward to read. Finger independence can be developed by slow practice in dotted rhythms, long/short and short/long, but wrist relaxation should not be endangered in trying to achieve this. Indeed, a vertical suppleness of hand and wrist can assist the musical shaping of note groups, so that they contrast legato and staccato touch effectively. For small hands, the LH jumps could prove easy to mis-judge; security here will be developed if the third finger's tip can maintain contact with its key, while octaves jump around it. A slight lateral wrist swing, when correctly timed, will allow controlled and relaxed access to the thumb and fifth-finger notes.

The variety of tonal directions – dots, accents and tenuto marks, singly or in pairs – allow the music's capricious character to emerge. The ability to convey them all, while keeping the music's unpredictability fresh, is the challenge here. Interpretations which manage to communicate this surprise element among all the sparkling energy will make the examiner smile.

C:2 Rakov Der Tag ist vergangen (The Day is Ended) (SG)

Although this beautiful piece appears simple on the page, considerable detail and control is required to bring it off. A tale seems to unfold among the piquant chords and strange turns of key. Managing these smoothly needs work, which students will find easier once they have an imaginative idea of the music's meaning. This in turn promotes a communicative performance.

When the notes are familiar, the best manner of gaining musical control is to separate the hands. This will enable your student to listen for legato flow wherever possible, especially in the inner parts (LH, bars 1–2, 17–18; RH, bars 5–8, 10–12). Neat fingering and sliding of thumb from one note to another is necessary; this additionally needs good tonal control to avoid unwanted bumps and gaps. Bars 9–10 may be hard to play accurately, with-out a sense of rushing when the hands cross. Gently placing these notes in chord form, with a reliable fingering, will help secure the keyboard geog-raphy and bring understanding of the harmonic continuity.

As the smooth texture gains fluency, the interpretation can become more personal. Even the simplest details, such as the RH repeated notes in bars 1, 2 and 3, need a purpose: are they repeating to insist on something, or do they fade away? How strong should the dissonant chords be: bitter-sounding, or simply sad? How much diminuendo is wanted at phrase endings? What sound is needed for the final floating chord?

C:3 Nicholas Scott-Burt Attitude! (SG)

From the composer's quote within the footnote, one would wish the posses-sor of such 'attitude' to be a friend; the music hints at a person who could never be boring! Good cheer is developed from the swing rhythm suggested in the tempo indication, and the plentiful inclusion of small musical details helps the personality and humour come across.

The rhythm contains a few potential traps, particularly in the placing of rests. The minim rest in the last bar is especially hazardous and bars 15–16 will need a good sense of underlying pulse. Unusually, this piece has a fairly even balance between the hands; both have melodic and harmonic roles throughout. Safe journeys from one chord to another in bars 4 and 7–8 need reliable fingering and separate-hands practice. As there are a number of changes in hand position at silences, pianists who enjoy playing this piece from memory might return to the score occasionally, to refresh their memory patterns. Overfamiliarity with a favourite party piece can sometimes lead to trips in performance, so the ability to pick up at any phrase in practice will help create security.

 The important musical markings give character and impact, but your student may like to add to them, in their own interpretation. This can help to bring imagination and a sense of immediacy to the performance, both of which would give listeners – including the examiner – enjoyable entertainment!

[C:4] Hywel Davies Adieu ⓢⓖ

Inspired by folk melodies in this 16-piece collection, Davies has devised textures and colours which give a warm sonority without the need for large hands or advanced technique. The falling shapes of the song phrases and the many chords which include the interval of a 7th contribute to its wistful melancholy. Nevertheless, an optimistic mood is also present, both midway and at the smilingly rising close. There are a number of important tempo directions in the music; these show the way towards the intended performance style.

Sweetly singing tone for the tune can develop if the fleshy pads of the fingertips find a feeling almost of squeezing the keys. However, it is important to avoid pushing each note down with hand or wrist weight, as this could cause unwanted heavy accents. The LH notes will need precise fingering to ensure that their two-part texture is maintained as smoothly as possible throughout. Care taken in playing LH upper notes gently will help develop a softly murmuring accompaniment.

To capture the folksong style most convincingly, a sense of improvisation could be encouraged. As long as the written rhythms have been safely mastered, a fairly free rhythmic flow will add this 'making-it-up' character. Moving the tempo forwards slightly within two-bar phrases can give direction; a moment to reflect, before continuing, enhances the poetic feel. These breathing spaces are doubly effective if preceded by a small decrescendo, although the f in bar 6 provides the one exception.

[C:5] Trad. Spiritual Swing low, sweet chariot ⓢⓖ

Singing spirituals gave comfort and encouragement to grossly overworked African slaves in foreign cotton, sugar and tobacco fields. The words were mostly religious and the melodies can be traced back over centuries to their African roots. Some became so popular that they still form a much-loved repertoire today.

This song's chordal nature invites quite a rich tone, helped by generous and relaxed weight in the forearms. Pedal use will contribute warmth, but care is needed to change exactly as each new harmony sounds, creating a smooth link without blurring adjacent chords. When the melody begins, it should be clearly projected, especially when the LH takes it up. Balance is important here: accompaniment notes/chords can form a gentle background, except perhaps in the case of the meaningful 'blue' chords which start in bars 10 and 18.

The style of this piece will come across best if there is a sense of momentum within each phrase to carry the line forward, but also a little breath between one phrase and the next. Achieving high marks in the exam may depend on moulding the melody musically; an example is the shading away implied by ♪ ♩. pairs (e.g. in bars 6 and 13), in which the shorter first note carries the greater weight. One important and lovely exception is the dotted crotchet B in bar 19, which benefits from an expressive sense of tenuto and prepares the unhurried approach to the song's finish.

C:6 Sarah Watts Curtain Call (SG)

The title here may refer to the closing part of a show, with the audience making their appreciation noisily heard. This cheeky number might be offered as an extra tune, to send listeners home thoroughly happy. Exploring recordings of swing will help your student discover the musical style.

The syncopations need to be precisely placed and all quavers will gain character from the requested triplet swing. A foot-tapping feel will spring from lively accents and from enjoying the places where show-off notes fall before or after the beats. The triplet style means that chords or notes tied across – in bars 4 and 6, for example – will jump in only fractionally before the third beat; they can gain an extra feel of swing by landing ever-so-slightly accented. Care should be taken not to hurry onto the notes following these tied ones, in order to preserve a strict pulse among all the rhythmic fun.

For a really sparkling performance, a special tone-colour might be found to highlight 'blue' notes: those which are a semitone lower than expected (e.g. the E♭ in bar 4, A♭ in bar 5). The song's big moment comes in bars 11-13; real theatricality here might find the tenuto octave leaps of the LH trying to steal the limelight from the melody. However, the wittiest bar comes just afterwards, in bar 14, where a complete change of colour will raise smiles all round, just before the throwaway ending.

GRADE 4

A:1 **Haydn** Minuet and Trio

Satin dance-slippers might be imagined tracing out this graceful Minuet below sparkling chandeliers and mirrored walls. The musical character flows from the contrast between light, crisp dotted rhythms and short gestures of rising or falling melody. Haydn has given basic dynamic markings; however, care might be needed to avoid playing too forcefully at *f* level. His expectation here would have been of a confident, but not harsh, sound.

Precise fingerwork will ensure that rhythm and articulation details remain clear. Occurrences of the opening motif can benefit from gently bouncing off the first and third notes; a relaxed wrist will help avoid harshness. Short legato groups (e.g. RH, bars 12–13, 23 onwards; LH, bars 5–6, 31–2) should be given musical shape, with care taken not to emphasize the last beat of bars. Singing tone in legato notes can be achieved by adding a little extra weight in the forearm, such that fingertips can feel a squeeze into the keys.

Elegance might be developed by phrasing off some second-beat crotchets in the Minuet (e.g. bars 3, 9–11) and any third-beat crotchets in the Trio. A touch of pedal on the quaver before bar 34 (across the bar-line) and to link the crotchet chords in bar 34 will help create a seamless legato at this expressive moment. Listening to music of the time on an eighteenth-century fortepiano could demonstrate what variety of colour and dynamic level is possible.

A:2 **J. L. Krebs** Praeambulum supra Jesu, meine Freude (Prelude on 'Jesus, My Joy')

Church music played a vital part in the lives of Baroque musicians. It formed a major source of income and, for many, was a genuine expression of their faith. Krebs used popular church tunes as the basis for his keyboard teaching pieces, rather as we enjoy arrangements of pop songs today. This piece weaves brilliant semiquaver patterns around a fairly well-hidden tune and allows the fingers to show off their athleticism.

Scales starting on the second semiquaver of beats need to begin without accent and can strengthen as they reach their high point. Evenness of fingerwork is paramount in this music and the broken-chord patterns may prove tricky to control. A slight lateral turn of the wrist, to keep it supporting the sounding finger, might be incorporated when practising these patterns slowly; this will become more fluid and subtle as the tempo increases.

A convincing performance should find room for considerable dynamic interest: often rising passages can crescendo, falling ones diminuendo. The music will gain in vitality wherever short groups of notes can be shaped (e.g. the end of bars 1 and 2) or accompanying quavers varied in articulation. Occasional pedal adds warmth to broken chords, but with the need for harmonic clarity borne in mind. The climactic bar 16 could rejoice in more generous pedal, with brief touches to colour the LH chords in bars 17–20, before the final line sends the Praeambulum away in a whirlwind of excitement.

[A:3] **Vanhal** Allegretto

This gently charming piece needs only a moderate tempo, but great attention to detail is required in order for it to come alive. The LH is in restrained accompaniment mode throughout and all expressive interest develops in the melody. The style is a shade Mozartian, so musical ideas might be gained from listening to opera arias such as 'Voi che sapete' from *The Marriage of Figaro*. That famous outpouring of the joys and hopes of young love, although somewhat slower in tempo, conveys the same warm-hearted tenderness as can be found in this Allegretto.

Experimentation with different fingerings might discover patterns which combine evenness with graceful shape. The treble line is very exposed, so absolute clarity and control will be wanted: scale passages need a really smooth passing-under of the thumb. Broken chords might benefit from slight lateral flexibility or rotation of the wrist, in order that all fingers give optimum tonal smoothness.

For a really stylish approach, details of articulation need time to be heard, for example where semiquavers are slurred in pairs (bar 25 etc.). Shading off the slurred pairs of quavers – the music's most important melodic element – will greatly enhance the meaningful feel. The phrases' repeating nature, while helpfully reducing note-learning time, offers a great opportunity to explore variety of touch and shaping. In a conversational way, some statements are confident, others more questioning, thoughtful or witty. The more imaginative your student can be, the more compelling the interpretation.

[A:4] **Clementi** Allegretto

As a reward for diligently practising scales and arpeggios, your students should find that most of this cheerful Allegretto falls easily under the hands. And for those less diligent or proficient, the piece presents an opportunity to brush up on finger dexterity! It is music typical of the Classical period, in which sparkling semiquavers and elegant phrasing will help produce a successful performance.

The only troublesome notes may be the broken chords in bars 20–22 and 56–8. These are slightly awkward 'tongue-twister' finger patterns and will need care to avoid stumbles or pulse loss. A top tip here is to extract the first five notes of bar 20, giving a small emphasis on first and last, bouncing lightly off the last, and repeating a few times with a relaxed hand. Another approach might be to extract the bar's second half, finishing on the first note of bar 21, and repeating similarly. Thirdly, students might play bars 20–22 slowly in dotted rhythms, long/short initially and then the harder short/long, to even out any weaknesses.

The most convincing performances will communicate enjoyment of the technical fireworks. The opening line might, for example, have a smooth LH and a smiling mood, followed by a detached LH (bars 7–22) in an exuberant continuation. Delicacy starting the *8va* run (bar 14) and a very crisp, quiet LH underneath will set up the boisterous and confident closing phrase of that half.

A:5 **Kirchhoff** Courante

The organist-composer Gottfried Kirchhoff studied with the same teacher as Handel. There are features in this lively piece which are reminiscent of the more famous composer's keyboard suites. The title Courante indicates a running dance in three time; its character might be captured by slightly lightening the last beat of each bar.

There are a few passages of tricky semiquavers (bars 5–8 and 28–31) which will need some slow preparation to achieve perfect flow. The highest notes in each of these bars might stick out unhelpfully, unless a slight wrist rotation can be developed to establish the greater importance of the first note of each four. This rotation will also assist in keeping the necessary rhythmic evenness, although the second and third beats should mostly be lighter than downbeats, if possible.

Despite the infrequent musical directions on the score, the examiner will be hoping to hear an imaginative approach to dynamic variety and interest. The second bar of each half, for instance, might become an echo, or bar 17 could perhaps be stronger than bar 16. The sequences that form much of the rest might find a sense of growing or reducing; each bar within them will also need shading as the melody goes up or down. Quavers that are not marked slurred could have some staccatos or be in slurred legato pairs, to add character. Students can enjoy choosing their own articulation schemes.

A:6 **Kuhlau** Allegro

The traditional elements of Classical sonatina writing are all to be found here: scalic phrases travelling gracefully across the keyboard, pretty broken-chord patterns, and 'horn-calls' to define the cadences. The section after the double bar-line is hauntingly beautiful, with surprise notes giving an unusual twist to the melody and some colourful harmonies or modulations.

The technical challenges are less those of rapidity than of evenness, both tonal and rhythmic, and it would be well worth giving the passagework extra attention where this is not achieved. At the flowing tempo, some LH quavers may also prove tricky: in bars 9–12 the hand should remain very close to the keys, leaning slightly towards the outer side, so that thumb notes protrude less than the more important bass notes. When the right degree of 'lean' has been found, the double 3rds should be easier to keep coordinated.

There is much scope for individual interpretation here. The character can vary considerably, according to the articulation plan and dynamic detail chosen for the crotchets. The quaver passages will also benefit from dynamic shading that is in addition to the composer's markings. A little pedal in bars 21–7 will warm the lovely harmonies, as long as quaver runs are left clean. This passage, especially, needs a really cantabile tone; the image of fingertips clinging onto a cliff edge may be helpful in conveying the means to achieve this.

B:1 H. Hofmann Scherzo (MMM)

The German composer Heinrich Hofmann was highly successful in his early years, writing orchestral works, operas and chamber music. He rose from poverty into wealth, and received honours from the state. However, as the century progressed and musical tastes changed, his music fell into obscurity. He is best known today for his piano music which he wrote for solo and duet.

Your student may take fright at the look of the notes on the page, but in fact the piece is not difficult. Taking the LH part first, it is found that the notes lie easily under the hand, and the suggested fingerings work well. It begins with a four-bar introduction before settling into the main melody after a pause. The light staccato chords of the accompaniment sound like the fluttering woodwind notes that Tchaikovsky loved to use in his orchestral music. They should be played with a relaxed hand dropping into the first chord and floating up from the second. In order to keep them in time, the beat could be tapped with the LH while practising.

Pedal has been indicated in several places and may also be used to join the first beat to the second in bars 2 and 4. The leisurely tempo can be eased a little in bars 8 and 28 to herald restatements of the principal theme, and in bar 16 to herald the start of the new section. The mood throughout should be happy and light-hearted.

B:2 **Schumann** Fröhlicher Landmann, von der Arbeit zurückkehrend (The Merry Peasant, Returning from Work)

There cannot be many pianists who have not played 'The Merry Peasant'. Schumann's wonderful collection of children's pieces is as enduring as the Romantic idyll of workers singing and dancing as they scrape a living from someone else's land!

A few adjustments to fingering may be made. There will be less movement of the LH's hand position if the thumb slides from B♭ to A in bar 3 and similar. Thus, from the upbeat A into bar 3 fingering would be 2-1 (on B♭)-2-5-1-1-2-5, etc. In bars 11 and 17 if the LH takes the first two inner chords with fingers 1/2 it is already in position to play the next two melody notes, and the RH, beginning with thumb, finds greater ease for its part. The pairs of accompanying quaver chords should always be lightly detached; a common mistake is to 'sit' on the second one.

Schumann tells us the piece is to be 'bright and cheerful' and the suggested metronome speed will provide plenty of vitality. The only dynamic mark the composer has given us is *f*, which appears at every statement of the main theme, but clearly more variety is needed. The theme itself should increase a little in tone as it rises to the top note, and then fall away towards the end of the phrase. And as suggested in the footnote, in bars 9–10 and 15–16 there is also the opportunity for a quieter level of tone.

B:3 **Žilinskis** Waltz in A

This beautiful slow waltz by the Latvian composer Arvīds Žilinskis is sure to be a popular choice. Like many Slavic composers of the twentieth century, his overtly Romantic music demonstrates a nostalgic longing for the past.

The pedal should be used throughout, changing only on first beats. However, the speed at which it is changed is crucial. Often players depress the foot too quickly, and in bars where there is a quaver on the first beat, as in bars 3, 5 and 6, the pedal must remain up slightly longer, so that the rest is audible. Conversely in bars 12 and 14 it will be important to catch the RH dotted minims before leaping to the high notes. The middle section is more passionate, lending itself to rubato and a fuller tone. It will be effective to play the second statement of its eight-bar melody at bar 25 like an echo, with spotlight now on the bell-like tenor line of the LH. The music should be allowed to fade before returning to the brighter first section.

The tempo is best felt as a slow one-in-a-bar so that the quavers flow along gently. The melody must always sing clearly, but the descending tenor line in the LH, which will be played by the thumb most of the time, is also important.

The sensitive balancing of these parts, together with skilful pedalling, will contribute to a rewarding performance.

B:4 Gurlitt Klage (Plaintive Cry) (MMM)

The key of F minor has long been used to express grief. In Gurlitt's beautiful study, the falling melodic shapes and appoggiaturas speak of sorrow. The first 16 bars take the form of a melody in AABA structure followed by a 16-bar variation that flows in semiquavers. The LH remains identical except for bar 27 and the last bar.

A lovely cantabile touch will be essential for the melody, preferably enhanced by pedalling. Changes of pedal on every crotchet beat will be sufficient to add bloom to the tone without blurring. If using the recommended edition, some adjustment to fingerings may be desirable. For instance, your student might prefer to start the melody with fingers 4 then 5, thus matching the second phrase – then to proceed as follows: (bar 6) 5-4-3-2, (bar 7) 4-5-4-3, (bar 8) 4-3, with the thumb playing all the lower notes.

In an exam situation it is easy to begin too fast. Mentally singing a bar or two of the semiquaver tune in advance will help set a manageable tempo. A metronome speed of ♩ = 84–8 will keep the quavers flowing without making the semiquavers agitated. The music's romantic nature suggests that a degree of rubato should be employed, and an easing of the tempo at ends and beginnings of phrases will help to illuminate the mood and structure. A diminuendo and poco ritenuto for the last two bars will allow the music to lapse into silence.

B:5 George Nevada Ninette's Musette (MMM)

Unlike the early form of the musette with its bagpipe drone or pedal notes, this delightful dance has more in common with the valse-musette, all the rage in Parisian cafes and dance halls during the late nineteenth and early twentieth centuries. The music was usually provided by accordions. *Ninette's Musette*, with its lilting melody, piquant harmonies and spicy added 7ths, was published in 1991.

The phrase structure is important. The 1+1+4+2 bars is the typical 'ready, steady, go' shape which is then answered by 1+1+6 to complete the first section. A certain amount of rubato is appropriate, but the phrases with four or six bars should always flow towards their cadence points. Some preliminary practice with LH and pedal will help to develop a secure accompaniment before adding the melody. It is essential that each crotchet bass note is sustained throughout the bar. Practising the melody supported by the first note in each bar of the LH will help your student to listen to the bass line and to judge the balance, too. The suggested pedalling works well.

The mood changes for the middle section. The key of C♯ minor, the bass moving downwards chromatically and the falling sequential repetition from bar 24 all contribute to a feeling of sadness and nostalgia. Doubling the melodic line with 6ths is another romantic gesture to be enjoyed. To round off this charming dance, the *D. S. al Fine* must be observed.

B:6   Tchaikovsky Mazurka   (MMM)

Generations of aspiring pianists have enjoyed Tchaikovsky's *Album for the Young*, and the Mazurka is a delight to play. The dance, which originated in a region near Warsaw inhabited by the Mazurs, spread westwards to the rest of Europe during the eighteenth century. At first glance this piece may seem rather long, but as in the original dance form, there is quite a lot of repetition. The mazurka's characteristic second-beat accents and dotted-note figures are immediately apparent, although the dot is replaced by a semiquaver rest!

In the first four bars, and similar places, pedal may be added – depressing it just after playing the minim and releasing immediately on the following first-beat quaver. This will add tone to the minim, assist the LH's jumps, but still allow the quaver to be staccato. Pedal must be employed sparingly, though, and never allowed to obscure staccato notes or rests. In the brighter middle section, accents shift to the third beats. Touches of pedal can help to join the slurred chords and highlight the accents except where there are staccato quavers in the melody, as for example in bars 19 and 23.

The dance is best felt as a lilting one-in-a-bar, ♩. = *c.*44. The marked dynamics are colourful, and in the middle section the crescendos should create excitement as the harmony returns to D minor by means of some dramatic Italian 6ths (the *sf* chords) and the first melody can reappear triumphantly.

C:1   Bjelinski Uzbuna (Alarm)   (MT)

This urgent-sounding, high-spirited piece suggests trouble at sea – man overboard? Despite its zany character, it calls for a clear sense of overview to allow each section to fit snugly together. Although the tempo should not flag throughout (alarms are persistent), students must pay attention to all the performance detail which captures the music's vibrancy and impetus.

For roughly half of the piece the hands play in alternation with each other, and this can lead to rhythmic disjointedness and bumpiness. Light wrists, with fingers positioned not too far into the keys, should alleviate this while encouraging nimble articulation. The semiquaver passage at bar 13 must not slow down, especially around bar 19, even if this means that the overall tempo is taken down a notch or two. Students might benefit from tackling the passage beginning at bar 28 early on, to ensure the LH crosses over without cluttering the RH.

It may be wise to fix on a couple of dynamic high-points – perhaps bars 26 and 40 – as this piece will lack its necessary zest if allowed to emerge with compressed dynamics and a uniform attack (the relatively sparing use of accents indicates the need to exercise restraint in this regard). The RH articulation introduced at the outset implies the subtlest of emphasis on the first note, while the LH can really enjoy its 'big tune' from bar 11 – which will sound all the more convincing against a gently insistent RH accompaniment.

[C:2] Ben Crosland Bow-Chicka-Wow-Wow (MT)

A 'wah-wah' guitar may not be familiar to your students, but a few minutes on YouTube should put that right. The effect applies mostly to the pairs of tenuto crotchets, such as at bar 3, where the RH needs time to hop over the LH. 'Moderate funk', taking due notice of the ¢ and the insistence on even quavers, sets the context for this quirky number.

Aside from the aforementioned hand crossings, the bulk of the technical hazards lie in rhythmic coordination. In each of the LH chords of bars 1–2 and 5 (and similar later) the top note C functions melodically as well as rhythmically. Your student should spot the subtle variation in notes between bars 10 and 26, and take time to sort out the marked finger transpositions at bars 13, 15 and 29, which are vital to realizing the musical texture. Pedal is not needed anywhere – indeed, important articulation detail will be lost by its injudicious use.

Encourage your student to feel the funky rhythms, and to hold back on the pace. The loudest section must surely come at the end, where the pulse nonetheless should be rock solid. The 'wah-wahs' will need that extra bit of bite to emerge convincingly, since the RH may not be accustomed to playing in this deeper register where the keys feel heavier. A good performance will be packed with pizzazz and kept lively with careful articulation in each hand.

[C:3] Trad. Russian Black Eyes (MT)

This attractive arrangement of a traditional Russian song bursts with expressive potential. To ensure its sections fit together effectively it will be worthwhile referring regularly to the metronome markings during learning. Care will be needed with tempo transitions, some of which are gradual (there are two accelerandos), others needing a decisive snap. The superbly doleful minor key LH melody at bar 4 deserves all the charming rubato your students can muster – but without upstaging the music's triple feel.

Effort taken over fingerings will be appropriately rewarded, not just in the initial LH cantabile tune, but in a couple of awkward RH corners, such as bars 19–20 and 48–50. What better practice for chromatic scales can there be than bars 44–8? The RH needs to take care in discreetly placing its chords from bar 4; some lie on the beat, others do not.

Bars 1–3 sound like an introduction to a song, and this piece will certainly suit students who possess a naturally expressive sense of melodic shaping. It also has much to offer those with flair, especially as they dispatch the *Molto appassionato* (where dabs of pedal might not go amiss), not to mention the impressive-sounding final nine bars; as always, evenness and control will earn more marks than a splashy, cavalier approach. The two *ff* occurrences, at bars 36 and 51, will sound all the more effective if carefully gauged from the starting dynamic of *p*.

C:4 Kabalevsky In The Gymnasium (MT)

Kabalevsky had an enviable knack of writing piano music which sounds impressive but is comparatively approachable to play. Though the title conjures up strenuous activities involving weights and rowing machines, it might be more helpful to imagine floor exercises and acrobatic tumbles. There are invitations to leap athletically – an intrepid vault of the horse at bars 1–2, perhaps? – and these accented chords at the beginning would benefit from a subtle crescendo towards the second bar, not a stolid, uniform attack.

Proficient fingers will prove vital, as Kabalevsky leaves no time to limber up. A controlled dispatch, with each section practised slowly and hands separately at first, will emulate a gymnast's effortless movement around the equipment. Emphasizing the contrasts in articulation between the hands – a highly persistent and important feature of the writing – will lend performances a chiselled, decisive quality; forward momentum is surely non-negotiable here. If students apply the same diligence to fingerwork as they would when playing Bach, keeping a 'still' hand, the piece should literally spring to life!

Paradoxically, the faster we play, the harder it is to place accents precisely where we want them, so your student should weigh up the marking *Allegro assai e marcato* circumspectly. There is the distinct risk of a performance becoming louder and louder if decrescendos are not followed. Clarity of purpose through the phrases (which are not marked in, so a moment with a pencil is indispensable) will do much to invigorate a performance.

C:5 Richard Lane The Penguin (MT)

Penguins cannot fly, and yet this piece is always confidently on the move. A self-assured walking bass will serve better than an indecisive waddle, and tasteful touches of spontaneity will greatly enhance the music's jazzy charm.

A few awkward chromatic figures invite a little sorting-out before the music's catchy rhythmic character can emerge, though systematic fingering and an occasional frugal dab of pedal will assist. The triplet crotchets at bars 9, 10 and 12 can be permitted a nonchalant air – likewise, the few instances where the RH meanders penguin-like down to the bass clef. It would be easy to overlook the unannounced changes from dotted to straight quavers at bars 6 and 19. If the LH thumb can be encouraged to move deftly onto the C at bars 5 and 18 this will greatly ease the sequences which follow. A charismatic effect can arise at bar 13 by gliding the thumb smoothly from F♯ to F♮.

A distinctive two-in-a-bar feel will coax out the penguin's personality, but too enthusiastic a pace may transform its convivial swagger into an ungainly canter. Careful observation of notated accents and dynamics should help students to trace out the ebb and flow of the laid-back melody. In particular, the *cresc.* through bars 9 to 13 requires patient grading to spotlight the *ff*, the loudest moment in the piece. At bar 18 the *pp* can trigger a dramatic build-up, emphasizing the music's amusing final cadence.

[C:6] Elissa Milne Foreign Correspondent (MT)

Foreign correspondents are known for their punctilious attention to detail and dogged pursuit of facts. However, the music's immediately alluring jazzy orientation might steer us more towards Pink Panther! The composer's metronome marking indicates that the music should have a two-in-a-bar feel, despite the time signature of $\frac{4}{4}$. A solid, unswerving tempo will serve your students admirably, until the nonchalant-sounding *molto rall.* with which the music concludes.

Aside from a couple of isolated bars (bars 16 and 24), which call for fastidious fingering and a careful appraisal of how the hands coordinate, most of the challenges arise from rhythmic subtleties. It will be helpful to look for where patterns repeat (bars 1–2 and 5–6, etc.) but also where they vary for interest (e.g. bars 8 and 20). The 'blue' acciaccaturas which crop up in the final lines are great fun to play, though their appearance may be alarming at first. Students should tuck them into the quaver runs without overworking the fingers, especially in bars 23 and 27.

'With accuracy' might just as easily be interpreted as 'with conviction'. As with many jazzy pieces, the score only provides the most essential clues to presenting a pleasing musical experience. The syncopations which heavily populate the piece invite extra edge, alongside enterprising dynamics, while the recurring quaver patterns, often doubled at the 4th to give additional colour, are to be played straight, not swung.

GRADE 5

A:1 **Purcell** Prelude   (MMM)

Although Purcell's output for harpsichord is not especially large, the set of eight Suites is of significance when viewing the development of the keyboard suite as a whole. He was a master of contrapuntal writing, and in several of the Preludes, especially this one, we have a foretaste of J. S. Bach.

The first task will be to decide on the articulation. As a general rule, quavers that move stepwise sound convincing played legato, while those that jump a 3rd or more will be best detached. Thus for the principal motif in bars 1 and 2 the first three quavers are staccato while the one on the third beat should be joined to the semiquavers. This motif or part of it is tossed about from hand to hand with entries a 5th lower and a 5th higher, and it appears in inversion at bar 12. After a three-bar dominant pedal, the motif returns in the tonic in bar 19, but begins to fragment until a new idea appears at bar 26. From this point there is a gradual build-up until arriving triumphantly at the final flourish of trills. Varied dynamics should be employed to highlight these important features.

The // sign for the trill is found in all of Purcell's keyboard music and is clearly realized here by the editor. The last note of the trill in bar 15 is timed with the LH's third-beat D, and in the last bar the ornament is an extended mordent played rapidly on the notes C-B-C. The dynamics are editorial, so there is no reason why your student should not have other ideas.

A:2 **Seixas** Allegro   (MMM)

Carlos de Seixas will be an unfamiliar name to many. Born in Portugal in 1704, he became a highly respected court musician and a friend of Domenico Scarlatti. It is supposed that much of his music was destroyed in the earthquake that devastated Lisbon in 1755, some years after Carlos's death at the early age of 38.

The score has been reproduced with very little editorial intervention, so before serious practising begins it will be necessary to decide on articulation and dynamics. For the RH melody the normal scheme of using legato only for those quavers that move by step (e.g. the ♫♫ groups at the fourth beat of bar 4, and second beat of bars 5 and 6) may be the best solution. All other quavers should be staccato, including most of those played by the LH, so that the lively nature of the music is realized. Some might like to slur those LH quavers that move by step (bars 9 and 11–12, for example). The ♫♫ group in bars 1 and 15 is like an ornament and should be played as quickly as possible, the hand floating up from the last note.

There is a lot of repetition that can make the music sound static, so it will be vital to vary the dynamics. There are opportunities for echo effects (e.g. in bars 2 and 4) and moments where a crescendo is implied – as in bars 11–12, perhaps arriving at f in bar 13. A rallentando at bar 24 will bring the piece to an impressive conclusion.

A:3 **Weber** Waltz in A (MMM)

Weber is best known for his operas, but he was a fine pianist and wrote four large-scale piano sonatas as well as concertos and smaller works for the instrument. At the time that he wrote his Six Waltzes it was fashionable to compose music that imitated the Turkish military bands. Some early pianos were fitted with drum, cymbal and bell effects operated by the 'janissary' pedal. The Trio section of this waltz, which is so like the final section of Mozart's 'Rondo alla Turca', indicates the use of this pedal.

The slurs over the LH accompaniment tell us to play legato, but the lines over the melody look more like phrase marks. The repeated notes in bars 1–2 and the pairs of notes that sound like the 'Mannheim sigh' in bars 4–6 need clarity. In the accompaniment your student might prefer to keep finger 2 on D throughout bars 5 and 6, and in bar 7, when the parts collide on E, the LH could take the note. It would be easier to play the crotchet B in bar 20 with the LH, too. A certain amount of pedal will add colour and sonority, but obscuring details in the articulation should be avoided, especially in the first section.

Compared with the mainly cheerful mood elsewhere, the Trio is quite fierce and one can imagine the clattering of the percussion instruments on those first beats! However, in bars 41–4 the texture should be lighter to provide a little relief from the battery. The suggested tempo of $\bullet$. = c.52 is ideal for bringing sparkle to this exhilarating dance.

A:4 **J. S. Bach** Prelude in E minor (MMM)

Not only are the 'little' preludes of J. S. Bach invaluable teaching material, they are all miniature masterpieces, tuneful but often challenging. The E minor Prelude is like a dance. The tempo is lively and best thought of as one-in-a-bar, with a metronome speed of $\bullet$. = 44–6.

Unless you have an urtext copy, details of articulation will vary from one edition to another. Feel free to start with just the notes, and discuss with your student where it might be suitable to put in slurs and staccato. A bright attack with crisp fingerwork is clearly needed for the semiquavers, whether they are chord shapes or scalic figures. It is the quavers that need the most thought, and in order to create the lively character many of them can be staccato. Slurs should be used to add emphasis to certain features. For instance, by slurring the first two quavers in bars 5 and 7 the falling sequence will be highlighted.

In bar 13 (and 15) a three-note slur followed in the next bar by a staccato quaver and two-note slur provides contrast for this new idea.

Where possible, ornaments should be included, but they must never disturb the rhythm. In bar 1 (and similar) the mordents should be on the beat and not allowed to delay the semiquavers, so practising first without them is useful. At the slow-practice stage it helps to place the first semiquaver with the third note of the mordent. Choice of dynamics provides an opportunity for your student to search for changes of mood and for sequences where terraced dynamics might be used.

A:5 **Mozart** Allegretto (MMM)

There is a pastoral flavour to this charming arrangement. Based on the finale of Mozart's Piano Trio K. 564, it assumes the character of a carefree country dance. Your student may feel daunted at first by the length of the piece, but as it is in sonata-rondo form, there is quite a lot of repetition. Encourage your student to discover how it is constructed.

Although pedal is not essential, it will not only add colour but will help to join some of the LH chords. For much of the time a simple movement down on the first beat and up on the second will be all that is needed. Legato pedal could be employed at bars 23–4 and 43–4 where there are no rests in the melody part. It is interesting to note that the bass line of the central episode (from bar 37) is written in dotted crotchets. Here it would be best not to employ any pedal at all so that the texture remains transparent. However, from bar 53, pedal will help to join the first beat's dotted-crotchet chords to the second beat.

Within the given dynamic marks, there is always a gentle rise and fall, and with a speed of $\downarrow$. = c.76 the music should dance gracefully. The rondo theme itself needs to swing along cheerfully in four-bar phrases, and perhaps to be differentiated in mood from the second subject (bar 16), to which it is closely related. At the central episode in C major your student can enjoy the more colourful harmony and chromatic flourishes.

A:6 **D. Scarlatti** Sonata in A (MMM)

Vitality and good humour abound in this Sonata. Agile fingers and lightness of touch will be needed, but it all lies comfortably under the hands and there are none of the scary leaps that Scarlatti so loves to employ. It would make an ideal choice for those with smaller hands.

The recommended edition is quite heavily edited with articulation marks and a few dynamics, but the result is stylish and works well. This is not to say that other interpretations are not possible. Examiners will always accept different ideas, especially with Baroque music, as long as they are consistent and in keeping with the style. For instance, the main cadences might be marked with detached notes in the LH. This would involve the two notes in bars 25, 30, 32 in the first half and bars 49, 54, 58 and 62 in the second. A short trill on the final note of each section would also be effective. There is no real need for the use of sustaining pedal in this texture, so repeated dotted crotchets need to be given sufficient length. The fingers should cling to the keys for as long as possible before releasing and replaying. This is especially important for the repeated 3rds.

There is quite a lot of repetition, and the use of echo or terrace dynamics could be effective. However, in bars 6–8 and similar passages there should always be a feeling of leading towards the top of the phrase, whatever dynamic level is being employed. A metronome mark of ♩. = 96–106 is quick enough to capture the sparkle of the piece.

B:1 Chopin Sostenuto in E flat

This waltz, by many pianists' most-loved composer, will surely be a popular choice. The notes and rhythms seem straightforward enough and dynamics are left entirely to the player's choice, so a trouble-free preparation might be assumed. However, this music is worthy of its great composer and hides musical, technical and communication challenges.

The first quest will be for true cantabile melodic tone. Flexible forearm weight, to support the hand, can feed through to a feeling that the fingertips almost drag themselves back along the key surface towards the player. In this way, lyrical lines can project with ringing sonority and their rising/falling flight may achieve the eloquence of a fine opera singer. In the second section, cantabile focus in the LH needs to be joined by fragments of well-projected RH melody in bars 18 and 22–4. However, careful listening might be needed at these points, so that notes lower down in the RH chords are not inadvertently emphasized. A slight outward hand-rotation may redistribute the tonal weight helpfully. Acciaccaturas are best incorporated lyrically, to keep the melody undisturbed by any sense of rush or tonal unevenness.

When performed with musicality, there will be a natural desire to pull the tempo back slightly at special moments, but the necessary and counterbalancing forward momentum is less often understood. Phrase endings, or a favourite note, chord or interval, might linger expressively in rubato style. Around any 'robbed' time moment, however, the tempo needs a little extra urgency; this ensures that the underlying pulse remains stable. Sensitivity to melodic and harmonic beauties can add the final touch of musicianship needed to stir the emotions of listeners.

B:2 | **Maykapar** Tarantella

Pianists with a taste for the fast lane will be happy in this *moto perpetuo* dance. It would suit those with small hands, as there are no large stretches and the dynamic level is predominantly quite soft. A delicate touch will enhance the floating-away nature of phrase endings and note pairs, although the final section offers opportunities for a more robust approach as the excitement increases.

Liquid flow will best be achieved by keeping the fingertips very close to the key surfaces. Slow practice in the early stages can help uncover any unevenness, particularly in the weaker fingers, so that an ultimately lively tempo is reached with a sense of ease. Phrase shaping can be worked on during this preparatory stage; harmonically, the emphasis often comes just after phrases start, with ensuing notes becoming lighter. The middle section, although remaining mostly soft, needs a more singing and sunny tone; graceful shaping towards each phrase's penultimate bar works well here. Louder dynamic levels should keep a warm tone, avoiding a tendency to sound shrill; the use of relaxed forearm weight and flexibility in the wrist will help establish the right touch.

The interpretation can find scope for colourful imagination in exploring the semitone intervals of the first line. Especially as the music becomes even more chromatic in the second half, where it builds in volume and pitch, the dance can develop a feeling of frenzy. The marking *con fuoco* suggests fiery enthusiasm as the main dance gets underway again. Perhaps the dancers have come really close together at this point, their energy focused before releasing outwards as the dance spins away to a dramatic close.

B:3 | **Vaughan Williams** Slow Air

Such is the rarity of piano music by Vaughan Williams that a chance to explore his more intimate style should be grabbed with all ten fingers! The restrained title betrays nothing of the beauties that lie within: a floaty tune gently unwinding, modal harmonies, yearning 7th chords and chains of parallel 5ths. Something of this musical flavour and peaceful melancholy could also be enjoyed in his *Norfolk Rhapsody No. 2* for orchestra.

The term *cantando* indicates where the main melodic focus should sing out at any point. However, in the somewhat contrapuntal texture, each 'vocal' line needs singing tone; this can be borne in mind right from the note learning stage. Choice of fingering needs to create seamless legato or meaningful repetition, depending on the situation. The editorial fingerings can assist this, and should be manageable by all but the smallest hands. Particularly in the inner parts of the texture, thoughtful control may be needed to join or repeat notes in a musical way. Discreet pedalling can help warm the sonority, but a carefully listening ear should monitor whether the clarity of lines is being over-smudged.

The music's exquisite fluidity arises from its subtle rhythmic nature; melodic or harmonic emphasis falls sometimes on second or third beats of bars and crotchets are often interestingly subdivided or tied over. Sensitivity to this improvisatory eloquence will allow the performance to develop poetry and expressive power; every note has its own relative importance within the line. Recalling instrumental timbres from the suggested Rhapsody might suggest tonal colouring to aim at, as solo lines, duets or trios contrast with lush chordal writing at the close of each section.

B:4 A. Beach The Returning Hunter SG

The American pianist Amy Beach was a successful composer at a time when women were not expected to perform in public. She wrote her Eskimo pieces based on Inuit folksongs, and gave them classical-type accompaniments. The themes in this piece have a distinctly outdoor feel, with march-like rhythms, regular phrasing and quite bold melodic repetitions. Sections tend to begin as if sung by the hunter alone, with his fellow adventurers joining in wherever the texture becomes more chordal. Two passages are more graceful, with pedal marked for extra warmth; one could imagine that here are the women-folk around the cooking pot, welcoming the hungry men back at the end of the hunt.

The rather fast tempo means that staccatos have to be crisp, and triplets agile. Louder chords and repeating quavers risk becoming over-strident in tone; playing enthusiasm could be guided here towards firm but very relaxed arm weight for chords, and lightening the tone for some of the repeated notes on weak beats. However, the weak-beat tenuto markings, or more gentle accents elsewhere, can help give rhythmic character. Slurred pairs of notes offer further interest, if shaded off expressively.

A sense of storytelling could help create a convincing performance. The middle section is especially colourful: the sinking passage of repeated quavers from high D (bar 36) seems to convey the brave hunter sitting comfortably down by the warm fire, with the ensuing quiet passage describing his tale of searching, anxiety, chase, and the eventual capture before a jolly homecoming. Of course, any suitable hunting story could work here, but the presence of an image is often enough to inspire lively communication.

B:5 Gedike Miniature in D minor SG

This 'miniature' piece is only so in length, not in musical challenges. Notes and rhythms are straightforward, but fine tonal control, flexible rubato and frequent full- or half-pedalling will be needed to capture all the beauty in this exquisite music.

Accompanying quavers can gain evenness by keeping close to the keys' surface, playing almost underneath the keys' resting level. Most melodic notes imply either growth or relaxation within the phrase, so sensitivity to tonal shading will produce the most musical results. Balance between lines in the texture could take time to achieve; in the outer sections, the LH needs to project clearly, while playing relatively softly and with meaningful shape. In bars 9–13 of the middle section the hands play a duet, with the accompaniment shared. Helpful practice here would be to omit the accompaniment and play only the melodic elements, including the RH thumb notes as bar 9 leads to bar 10. As tonal control improves, the duetting lines can acquire singing expressivity, which should be preserved when the full texture is later reconstructed. Bar 10 holds a particularly telling moment, when the tune passes from a crossed-over LH to the RH's upper line; a fine-tuned listening ear can judge the exact tone needed for a seamless flow.

After the concentration needed for this preparatory work, a freeing of the mind and consideration of the music's emotional message will lead to a communicative performance. Listening to a few songs by Rachmaninov, or a British contemporary of Gedike, might encourage your students to compose words for the melody, or to imagine a story that they feel they can 'tell' when they play.

B:6 **Grieg** Waltz in E minor

A delicate Romantic style is evident here, with fleeting emotions and a sense of melancholy poetic expression. Echoes of Grieg's *Peer Gynt* suites can be heard and lovers of Chopin's waltzes should encounter much to delight them.

Successful accounts of this piece will convey all the composer's performance details and find true cantabile tone for the main melody. A pedalling plan of changing after the next bar has just begun is generally appropriate. However, bars 2, 6, 11 and 13 contain extra harmony changes, so more frequent pedalling is needed. Bars 17–32 introduce a new mood; flexible RH wrists can help to shade the tone in those floating gestures. In this section, pedal could be lifted completely at the third beats, or omitted altogether in the staccato LH bars. Your student might explore rubato at points of special harmonic or melodic beauty, always remembering that stretching of the pulse for a particular moment should have a corresponding push forwards before or afterwards, so that the underlying pulse is secure.

Communicating the music's character will need a firm conviction about what might be happening. The Presto middle section, for example, could give the impression of other dancers in the ballroom seeming to blur, as the waltzing couple spins lightly and with abandon. A brief pause to steady the giddiness leads back to the first tune, but here the harmony is subtly different and strong passions seem to develop. It would suit the Romantic style if the interpretation of the musical details could find new character or meaning in this final section, even though the notes almost match the opening 16 bars.

C:1 **Tan Dun** Staccato Beans

This is music full of fun and energy, with a distinctive folk idiom. The composer is recalling childhood memories and the piece has an irresistible feel of play and freedom. There are also moments of child-like impatience – perhaps the odd toy is thrown down or a door slammed! The writing is tonal but the key often ambiguous until the sudden end of the games in an emphatic D minor. There are a few stretches, but this piece should be suitable for hands of all sizes.

The tempo is quick, but it should not feel like one-in-a-bar. More important is stability in the rhythm plus energy and precision in the fingerwork. For this the touch should be positive and firm with full clarity achieved at all dynamic levels, and the staccatos will need bounce in both fingers and wrist in order to be crisply articulated. Practising with a metronome will assist in gradually building up tempo, while ensuring that the pulse stays steady.

A wealth of detail, particularly relating to articulation, is given in the performance directions. Time and care should be taken to assimilate these as they contribute greatly to the character. Sometimes staccatos and slurs are combined, giving opportunity for further variation in the touch. The dissonant RH chords should sound really edgy, observing each *sf*, and the dynamic range is huge, with sudden changes as well as crescendos. Interestingly, there is not a single diminuendo. It isn't often justified simply to hit a note as hard as possible but, given that the final low D follows an ***fff***, and is accented, your student can relish doing exactly that!

C:2 **Shostakovich** Gavotte

Shostakovich creates a vivid scene. One can picture the costumed dolls as they step and dance around the stage and there is a delightful mix of slightly mechanical movement and spontaneity in the writing. A child-like quality pervades the melodic lines but humour and sophistication abound here too – witness the rapid and skilful harmonic shifts so typical of the composer and the clever, inventive bar 48 leading into the final reprise, at the end of which the dolls trot happily off stage, the last one giving a little jump as it disappears.

Quick changes of articulation are called for, and those such as in bars 6–7 will need slow practice to develop the precise control needed. This is also true of the legato 3rds and other double notes in the RH, which present different fingering options. Most technical challenges are in the treble part but the LH has some leaps to negotiate, and keeping the hand-shape stable in bars 9–10 and 17–22 will aid accuracy. The grace notes will work best if they sound just before rather than on the beat.

 The dynamic range need not be very wide, but markings in the score should be observed closely and the balance weighted in favour of the treble. There are choices to make too. The crotchet sequences in bars 1–3 and elsewhere, for example, could be detached but not too short, mimicking the dolls' slightly jerky movement, while contrast is provided by smooth joining of the minims and semibreves in the bass. The repeated slurs in bars 15 and 23 should sound quite insistent, and the characterful accents will benefit from a positive emphasis.

⌊C:3⌋ Stephen J. Wood Cool (NO)

This laid-back piece is ideal for a first try at jazz style, as well as suiting those already versed in the idiom. The melody meanders up and down with a relaxed flow while the lower parts fill in the texture with catchy rhythm and harmony. The trick here is to get all the detail into an easy, unfussy-sounding context. It will help to imagine a jazz trio: the saxophonist, eyes shut, effortlessly projecting the tune while the keyboard and bass players slot in with both subtlety and distinctiveness.

Underlying the casual mood must be a firm grasp of the rhythm – encourage your student to be diligent in counting everything carefully. While the music is being assimilated, thinking in a broad two-in-a-bar will remove any mechanical element. The notes are not too difficult but chords must be articulated with all notes sounding simultaneously, and voicing the chromatic slides such as in bars 3 and 21 will add spice to the mix!

 The melody needs cantabile sound, positive fingerwork and expressive shaping, pointing out the accents but never with undue force. Until the instruction to the contrary near the end, the pairs of quavers should be swung. The pedal needs judicious use: long melodic notes which can't be held by the fingers can be sustained with pedal, but wherever possible your student should avoid blurring the harmonies and clouding the texture. The music could slow right down at the close, with the pedal held down from the end of bar 49 as the melody climbs softly away into the night.

⌊C:4⌋ Gershwin Summertime (NO)

In this most famous of songs, from Gershwin's opera *Porgy and Bess*, a mother lovingly tells her child that summer living is easy, and while some day wings will be spread and the nest left behind, for now there is nothing of concern with Daddy and Mummy standing by. Gershwin's music is lyrical and profoundly expressive, evoking also the heat, haze and languor of the American

Deep South. Encouraging your student to learn the lyrics and listen to the original music will foster understanding of the affectionate mood and gentle blues style.

Nothing is fast-moving, although it mustn't sound static, and the challenge is all about creating beautiful sound and seamless lines. Melodic projection is paramount, from the moment the introduction ends midway through bar 7. Fingers should press deep to the base of the keys with fingerings organized to join everything as smoothly as possible. Accuracy in rhythmic detail is also important, but there can be plenty of flexibility, and time may be taken over the potentially awkward movements in bars 15 and 33.

Imaginative use of the pedal will add a lot of colour and tonal interest, and experimenting here will reveal which sequences of notes work without changes. Some judicious blurring of texture creates atmosphere, but choices should be made carefully. The music probably need never be louder than *mf* but there should be rise and fall within the phrases with lower parts blended so that long melodic notes sustain (e.g. in bar 8). The high F♯s and G♯s can have a bell-like ping, and at the end the hands may roll gently over the final chord, leaving the parental smile hanging in the still air.

C:5 Nikki Iles Up on the Hill (NO)

This charming, pastoral piece takes a relaxed stroll in the spring sunshine, a few dissonant intervals and syncopations adding a jazzy flavour to the lyrical style. Much of the material is repeated, with a few variations in register and rhythm the second time, before a coda – in which, perhaps, the rambler pauses to rest and take in the view. The pace is unhurried but the phrases need flow and direction with accurate realization of the rhythmic subtleties.

Flexibility and suppleness in the hand will be essential for success in this piece. The RH part has a significant amount of harmonic material, as well as the main melody, and projecting the upper notes while holding the lower ones for their full value will need practice. Careful fingering choices will help achieve this, and also in sustaining smooth legato lines; using the thumb for the two lowest notes in bars 1, 16 and 17 might work well. Much of the music would benefit from the textures and colours gained by using the pedal, and in some places sustaining the bass notes is nearly impossible without it, but care needs to be taken to avoid blurring the melody.

Only gentle gradients feature in this outing, and phrase shaping should reflect this, using expressive but moderate rises and falls. Notes with tenuto lines above or below are to be considered: some ask for extra cantabile in the melody, but others stress rhythmic and harmonic features, such as in bars 27–8. The close can be lingered over, with enough tone on the top F to sustain it right to the end.

C:6 **Kabalevsky** Novelette

Kabalevsky tells an expressive and mournful tale, the minor tonality and the bass line's steady trudge suggesting a rather melancholy journey. There is raw emotion, too, in the biting dissonances and the volume that builds towards the middle of the piece as powerful recollections are stirred, before the passion subsides and an air of resignation pervades by the end. The characterization is reminiscent of Schubert's Lieder writing, and yet the dark harmonic colours are hallmarks of the composer's native Russia. Students will need to be able to reach the pedal comfortably and stretch an octave, but there are no other obstacles to tackling this characterful music.

The pedal can be used throughout; one change at the start of each bar works well, although two changes might be preferred in bars that are more melodically chromatic (e.g. bars 16 and 18). Lifting the foot exactly as the fingers go down before quickly pressing the pedal again will maintain smooth joins. Equally smooth must be the legato touch in the RH, with carefully planned fingerings and slow practice of each phrase in isolation needed to master the 3rds.

The piece has a huge tonal range; it will be important to project the top line at all dynamic levels and shape each phrase expressively. The sound should never be harsh, even at the climax, and slightly stressing the lined notes will add pathos to the mood. Encourage your student to find particular points of beauty, such as the unexpected shafts of sunlight in the major chords of bars 19 and 44, or the change in melodic register to the middle of the texture near the end.

GRADE 6

A:1 **J. S. Bach** Invention in A minor

J. S. Bach's Inventions provide the gateway to playing and understanding his writing at a deeper level. The interweaving melodies, imitation and coordination between the hands give great satisfaction to performer and listener alike. As mentioned in the footnote Bach wrote his Inventions as lessons in 'how to arrive at a *cantabile* style of playing'. Written just under 300 years ago, the lack of dynamics might encourage imaginative interpretation in some students, while others will need guidance.

To accomplish this piece successfully, the hands need to be equally weighted in their dexterity and evenness. The editorial metronome marking is a standard tempo, but it is advisable to start much more slowly and build up to it. Articulation contrast could be addressed by beginning with legato semiquavers and detached quavers, ensuring good balance between the hands, but bringing the more dominant melody to the fore (e.g. the LH entry at bar 6). Bar 19, in which both hands play semiquavers together, will require slow and even practice, and a crescendo in the LH's final rising 6ths will result in a triumphant finish.

A lively tempo should herald the opening, with nimble fingerwork and imaginative dynamics: block dynamics, graded, echo phrasing, and so on. It may be helpful to discuss the type of instrument for which Bach wrote his keyboard music. Certainly not the piano, this is likely to have been the clavichord, an expressive, quiet instrument which could vary its dynamic level from *ppp* to *mf*. A more enthusiastic, informed and stylish performance may well be encouraged if your student has the opportunity to explore the sounds of such an instrument.

A:2 **Handel** Courante

As a young man, Handel wrote many keyboard works before travelling through Europe and eventually making England his home. He was well versed in the expressive qualities of the harpsichord, as he played it in the opera orchestra in Hamburg. Expression on the harpsichord was left to the skill of the performer, who could show the musical qualities of this 'plucked' instrument through articulation, speed of attack, length of holding notes, ornamentation and choice of manual.

A strong sense of pulse, with weaker second and third beats leading towards the stronger first beat, will facilitate the phrase direction needed. To achieve the running semiquavers and feeling of a dance the tempo most definitely has to be swift; however, there will need to be extensive practice at a slower tempo than the suggested metronome marking to encourage evenness in the frequent, rapid thumb transitions (1-2-1-2 in bar 9, for example). In these sections where the melody alternates from high to low a charming distinction can be made through experimentation with tone and dynamics. Indeed, throughout this piece your student can vary expression and tone by exploring block dynamics, echo phrases, sequences, and rises and falls.

The RH generally needs to dominate the LH, showing the shape and outline of the regular phrases, ensuring the importance of crisp, neat ornaments with curved fingers and a lift of the wrist at the end of each bar. Teaching an understanding of the harpsichord will help to make this piece come to life; you might also illustrate the shorter compass of its keyboard by placing two objects either side of a four-octave range.

[A:3] **Mozart** Rondo

Following his father's death in 1787 Mozart wrote only three more piano sonatas before his own death in 1791. He was struggling both financially and emotionally, yet produced this delightful sonata in 1788. Written 'für Anfänger' (for beginners), it shows Mozart's characteristic articulation, structured phrasing and memorable melodies.

From the outset the performer is confronted with capricious double 3rds, to be played with curved fingers and a strong chordal shape. These 3rds are deceptive, however, so for a stumble-free performance the tempo needs to be based on the final semiquavers. Articulation choices will define the phrase, therefore it is essential that the wrist is loose, using directional weight to lighten ends of phrases and shape the cantabile lines.

The Alberti-bass sections, combined with even RH semiquavers, are some of the most problematic passages in the movement, but encouraging your student to practise the LH in chords and to use a light RH finger staccato will help. The repeated notes at bar 9 could be played either with a repeated finger or with 4-3-2-1, depending on the hand type. Maintaining curved fingers from bar 60 – and aiming for a smooth transition when moving between hand positions – will allow the closing passagework to sparkle.

The movement starts on an upbeat, which is the key to getting the correct phrase inflection. Pedal might be added to colour chords, and it is possible that Mozart's title 'for beginners' indicates his intention that students add their own dynamics. Certainly the rondo theme needs a rise and fall in its running semiquavers, followed by a confident final *f* once the closing passages have been mastered.

[A:4] J. S. Bach Andante

William Whittaker (1876–1944), an examiner for ABRSM and a great friend of Holst, was an avid Bach lover and successful arranger, as reflected in this piece originally written for organ. A 'pastorella' was a short four-movement work associated with Christmas; it often contained a drone bass similar to the sustained bass line which dominates this composition under the aria-like melody.

The powerful sentiment of the music needs to be addressed through encouraging a warm, rounded tone, achieved by using the wrist to play into the keys. You might lift the piano lid and show your student how the double escapement action works, with a view to demonstrating the LH playing into the keys without lifting them fully, keeping the dampers released to achieve a ringing sound. The RH melody will then soar above the sustained LH chords adhering to Whittaker's performance direction (*il basso sempre sostenuto*). Time spent on ornaments, describing their decorative purpose, will help your student communicate the intrinsic richness of the melody. The repeated RH notes require a change of finger on the repeated notes (e.g. at bar 4) to achieve the articulation marked.

Use of pedal is desirable to colour and connect where a legato is not possible. However, the melody needs always to be lucid and not blurred, and insisting on practice without pedal first, to achieve a finger legato, is advisable. A slight rubato leading to bar 49 will heighten the musical intensity prior to the lamenting, final phrases. Controlling the long, sustained dynamic progressions and grading the phrases carefully will enthuse the able student to really explore the deep emotional content of the piece.

[A:5] **Beethoven** Andante

Take a trip into Beethoven's melancholy world with a unique brooding opening in G minor. The opus number is deceptively suggestive of his middle period, when the turmoil of his hearing loss gripped his writing; however, it was written before this time, in around 1797, and published later, arguably with a pedagogical objective. Classical sonata form prevails, with glimpses of Romantic characteristics in the combination of vivid contrasts, long soaring melodies, and the darker harmonic potential of the minor keys.

The movement's beauty lies in the Beethovenian cantabile, which requires a deep touch and impeccable finger legato – particularly in the LH's double 3rds at the opening. The flowing Alberti-bass sections in the second subject need good coordination, and the RH melody should soar, with even, shaped semiquavers. The unisons at bar 34 herald the development and the first *f* of the piece. Nimble, curved fingers will help execute the demisemiquavers, and leaning on the outer fingers will facilitate the legato octaves from bar 50, which should project well. Encourage sinking into the keys on each *sf* in bar 92, before maintaining excellent finger contact and control in the final *pp*.

The musical maturity within this sonata can be explored by taking time with and tapering off phrase endings. Space would be beneficial at cadences and section endings, for example adding a delicate rubato to the expressive chromatic octaves that lead into the recapitulation at bar 64. Keeping aware of the andante marking, maintaining good tone, and capturing the drama and contrasts are also important. The various articulation markings should be followed, while simultaneously bearing in mind melodic direction and length.

⟨A:6⟩ D. Scarlatti Sonata in F

Principally during his time in Lisbon and Madrid, Scarlatti wrote a staggering 555 piano sonatas, apparently for Maria Barbara, daughter of the king of Portugal and later the Queen of Spain. He was responsible for her harpsichord lessons, thus creating a wealth of compositions, which stand at the core of piano repertoire. The autograph manuscripts of Scarlatti's sonatas have never been found, though the Kirkpatrick catalogue lists them in what is believed to be chronological order. While the date of composition is unconfirmed, this sonata contains the classic hallmarks of Scarlatti, such as binary form and two-part writing.

Scarlatti's style warrants crisp ornaments, which can be extended in the closing cadences. Rhythmic lift can be achieved by contrasting short crotchets and legato quavers, and the hands will need careful balancing throughout with even and accurate quaver playing. The expressive student can explore the echo phrasing at bar 15 and the similar sections thereafter. The contrasting second section at bar 20 throws the sonata into minor tonality, calling for a more legato, well-rounded touch to express the darker sentiment. The LH octaves in the closing phrase of this section (and in bars 94–7) can be practised with the thumb leading the direction of the hand before adding the fifth finger.

Since the keyboard sonatas were originally for harpsichord, describing the instrument will help your student understand the block dynamics that result from playing on different manuals and stops. Articulation provides the key to expression, with longer notes denoting a more *espressivo* tone and minor tonality while an energetic, nimble tempo will allow the glittering passagework to sing through.

B:1 Gade Scherzo

Niels Gade was the foremost Danish composer of his generation. His works include eight symphonies, a violin concerto and numerous works for piano. Like his friend and colleague Robert Schumann, Gade gave many of his piano pieces titles that were inspired by different branches of the arts, like literature, dance or, in this case, painting. This delightful Scherzo comes from a set of pieces called 'Watercolours'.

Agility and lightness of touch with the arms feeling buoyant and well-supported will be essential. The opening figure with its rapid finger substitution on each B (bars 1 and 2) will need special care; some players may find using fingers 2-5 more comfortable than 3-5. Only a few pedal marks are given, but there is scope for more. A touch from the first quaver beat to the second in bars 3, 7 and similar will mark the descending bass notes and add a little bloom to the quavers in the melody. In bars 10–15 the pedal should be changed on every crotchet and quaver. In order to manage the rapid movement of the foot, the pedal should not be depressed further than absolutely necessary.

When it comes to managing the dynamics, the delicacy of watercolour paintings should be borne in mind. More than half of the piece is at *p* level, and the texture must remain transparent even in the louder passages. The *una corda* pedal would be appropriate for the last three bars. Listening to a good performance of Mendelssohn's *Rondo Capriccioso* (the second section) or the Scherzo from *A Midsummer Night's Dream* will help your student to capture this special sound-world.

B:2 Merikanto Valse lente (Slow Waltz)

The Finnish composer Oskar Merikanto is probably best known for his songs and church music, although he wrote in excess of 80 miniatures for the piano. He was almost certainly overshadowed by his great contemporary, Sibelius. Nonetheless, this beautiful slow waltz is one of Merikanto's most frequently played pieces.

The dynamics should rise and fall to reflect the arch-like shape of the melody, and in order to ensure a smooth line in bars 1, 2 and similar the sound at the end of the dotted crotchet must be matched by that of the following quaver. At bars 17–24 extra care will be needed to make the inner melody sing. As with any waltz, a relaxed and flowing LH will be important in order to provide a secure support for the melody.

Sustaining pedal will be required throughout the piece, regardless of the staccato marks which simply indicate the type of touch to be employed. The easiest solution is to pedal right through the bar, changing on every first beat, except in bar 5 where there is a new harmony on the third beat. This will work even in the quicker middle section where the texture becomes thicker.

However, the pedal could be released on third beats in those bars that have a crotchet rest in the accompaniment. This would provide some welcome contrast. In bars 49–52 the pedal can sustain the whole of the rising figure.

The frequent directions for tempo change indicate a form of rubato and must be observed. The *molto rit.* over bar 47 should continue through the silent bar, too, before the *poco vivo* scampers away to the final cadence.

B:3 **Skryabin** Prelude in E (MMM)

Skryabin's contribution to the piano repertoire is of considerable importance. Born in Moscow in 1872, he was a brilliant pianist and devotee of Chopin, whose music was a great inspiration. The set of 24 Preludes is based on the same key system as Chopin's own Preludes. However, the harmony and tonality in the Skryabin set is more unusual. In this one there is a strange mixing of E major and C♯ minor.

The successful balancing of the LH melody with the countermelody, heard at the top of the texture, is crucial. It will be worth taking time to practise these two lines as a duet before attempting to fill in the harmony. Some of the chords are quite widely spaced, but there are several places where the LH can easily help out. For instance, in bars 5, 14 and 16 the lowest note of each third-beat chord can be taken by the LH thumb. Any other wide chords may be spread. The use of pedal will be essential. A change on each crotchet beat is all that is needed, except in bar 2 and similar, where the pedal should be held through the bar. In the last two bars the score suggests that the pedal should be changed in order to clear the low E, but if students cannot stretch a 10th, they should simply keep the pedal depressed.

The style is very expressive and emotional. The rubato indication is clearly shown in the score by the tenuto lines (bar 1) and the ritenuto marks that hold the music back a little but only for a few beats. The melody lines must always sing with a warm, rich tone.

B:4 **Cervantes** Los tres golpes (The Three Strikes) (MMM)

The meaning of the title, 'The Three Strikes' (or 'hits'), is intriguing. It might be based on a folksong, of which there is more than one, or even on the famous Dominican breakfast dish of eggs, salami and fried cheese! Whatever it might be, this most attractive Cuban dance will make an excellent choice for the exam or a concert.

Performance details including pedalling, articulation and dynamics are all clearly marked in the recommended edition. Grace notes in bars 2 and 10 should be played before the beat, but the acciaccaturas (bar 7 etc.) should be snapped on the beat, played with the lower of the two notes they precede. Time should be spent learning how to negotiate the leaps in bars 19–20; your student would be advised to memorize these so that eyes can remain on the keyboard here. Full value should be given to the rests in bar 28, and the chords that follow must be spaced out. Once the syncopated rhythms have become natural and relaxed, and one or two awkward corners mastered, the piece does not present any great technical difficulties.

The rhythms seen together in bar 2 are typical of the tango and habanera, and found throughout the piece. So, too, are three significantly marked chords (the three strikes?) that first occur at the cadence points in bars 7–8 and 15–16. Strong accents need to be employed for these chords, which become more frequent and insistent. The crescendo in bar 30 leads to *sub. p a capriccio* and a slyly altered version of the strikes. Could this be the musical equivalent of a wink?

B:5 J. N. Hummel Andantino in A flat (MMM)

As a child prodigy, Johann Nepomuk Hummel studied with Mozart, making his first public appearance at the age of nine. Later he was to become a renowned virtuoso pianist and teacher, and in 1828 produced a very successful teaching method in which he developed new ways of fingering and playing ornaments. The beautiful Andantino in A flat comes from this treatise.

The piece is in ABA form and begins with a calm and expressive melody which is only briefly disturbed by a shift to the tonic minor (bar 9). Here the dynamics are more extreme, hinting at the drama to come. The ability to bring out the top note of the chords, so that the melody sings clearly, and making sure that the dotted-note patterns do not slacken into triplet rhythm are two of the essential features of a convincing performance. Pedal must be employed carefully, never obscuring rests or staccato notes: for instance, in the first two bars, it can connect first to second beat and third to fourth. In bars 4 and 8 legato pedalling will join the three chords there.

An awareness of key colour will be important. For instance, notice the change of key when the tonic A♭ shifts enharmonically to G♯ and the music plunges *ff* into E major at bar 17. Here a brief but turbulent middle section passes through D♭ minor and B♭ minor before relaxing onto the dominant of F minor in bar 22. Thereafter it gently calms down before returning to the opening theme. Like Haydn before him, Hummel treats the recapitulation to variation with a flowing semiquaver melody weaving above the familiar harmony. With so many changes of mood, this is music to relish.

B:6 Martinů Pohádka (Fairy-Tale) (MMM)

Many composers, artists and writers have drawn inspiration from the characters of the Italian *commedia dell'arte* theatre. In Martinů's set of 14 pieces, he features Pierrot, Columbine and Harlequin, as well as some unnamed puppets.

✋ The first section presents few problems as long as the LH takes all the notes in the treble part that are shown with downward stems. It is also important to keep the key signatures in mind to avoid any incorrect accidentals creeping in. Pedal will be needed to bind the texture, but with care taken that the crotchet rest in bar 2 (and similar) is heard! Most of the challenges are found in the Trio. Mastering the LH part requires slow practice and a lot of patience. An alternative fingering may help towards fluency. Starting with the given fingering of 1-2-5, your student might try 2-1-4 for the next figure (bars 35–6), then, with fifth finger on the dotted minim, fingers 1-2-3 (bars 37–8), and finally 2-1-4 until the end of the passage. The accents should be positively marked, the conflicting rhythms suggesting some agitation. Only when the LH feels secure should the RH be added. Bearing in mind that the Trio is *poco vivo*, the tempo at the Moderato opening might be ♩ = 116–20.

🎨 We do not have the story of this fairy tale, so your student may wish to invent one as the piece takes shape. The opening chord that is repeated several times sounds bell-like, and in the middle section the LH's revolving figure with its shifting accents seems to suggest the uneven whirring of a spinning wheel – a recurring theme in fairy tales.

[C:1] **Bartók** Joc cu bâtă (Stick Dance) (TB)

🔑 This dance presents a vivid portrait of Eastern European peasant life, solidly earthbound, yet also sensitive and joyous. The melodic line, with its modal flavour, has its roots in the folk tradition, yet the harmonies provide a twentieth-century perspective. Bartók's meticulous attention to detail, indicating every nuance of tone and phrasing, offers many clues to the subtleties within the piece. Each of the two broad phrases is repeated, the changes of harmony providing a fresh view of the melody.

✋ Practising the LH alone, moving across the keyboard in an arch shape, will help accuracy in the leaps. The suggested chord fingering, often designed to allow smooth transitions between chords, may need some organization. Although various choices in pedalling are possible, the priority should be to sustain and enrich bass harmonies, while always allowing clarity in the RH detail. Initially subdividing into quaver beats may be necessary for sorting any intricacies in the RH rhythm, especially the triplet figures and semiquaver/demisemiquaver differentiation.

🎨 The composer distinguishes clearly between accents/sforzandos/tenuto marks, and staccato dots/wedges, each of which has its own level and quality of attack. Ornaments and faster detail give a spontaneous feel to the melodic line, as if improvised, and gauging the amount of tone at the start of the crescendos will allow maximum impact. Sonorous bass notes and tight rhythmic control immediately establish the strength and rhythmic solidity of the opening. A change of mood, gentler and more subtle, occurs at bar 17. There is scope for slight lingering to cherish the harmonies' quietest moments, and the *poco allargando* in the final bars provides space for enjoying the full richness of keyboard sonority.

[C:2] **Melville A. Leven** Cruella de Vil

'I love furs. I worship furs' – so says the famously wicked Cruella de Vil, who kidnaps Dalmatian puppies in order to make coats from their young fur. The sophistication and cunning of this character, whose name is a subtle adaptation of 'Cruel Devil', is readily apparent in the 1961 film *101 Dalmatians*. In this song transcription, the vocal line is woven into the piano texture, and the chromatic harmonies that frequently creep downwards contribute towards the sinister, wily mood.

Although relaxed, easy-going swing rhythms, as if improvised, are the ultimate goal, establishing an unwavering four-in-a-bar pulse is an essential part of the initial learning process. Responding to your student's preferred learning style will ascertain whether feeling the rhythm, possibly through singing, or understanding visually the relationship between the syncopations and the pulse is the best way forward. Initially practising without pedal highlights the need for a fingering which will sustain the two-voice texture. Thereafter, however, selective use of the pedal will allow clarity to the phrasing detail while helping to join the chords.

Each statement of the main tune offers scope for a contrast of approach. The smoothest legato line will characterize the slinky character of the opening, with offbeat accents and rests punctuating the 'vocal' line, while imitating the sonority of a bass saxophone will highlight the change of register at bar 13. The more upbeat middle section from bar 21, with its slurs across the beat, might benefit from a little more pace, whereas the f section beginning at bar 28, complete with RH tremolos and stride bass, turns the piece into a big showbiz number for a few bars.

[C:3] **Karen Tanaka** Masquerade

The title suggests disguise and elusiveness, perhaps masked figures at a party. Rhythmic ambiguity which prevails in the outer sections – the triple flow of the RH pulling against duple patterns in the LH – contrasts with the more straightforward rhythmic flow midway. Further variety is provided by the exploration of different registers of the piano between sections. This piece is ideal for small hands, and the most essential requirements for an effective performance are an alert sense of rhythm and confidence over the whole keyboard.

A crisp staccato touch, keeping the fingers close to the keys and listening for absolute evenness of attack, drives the LH forward at the outset. Slow practice will help to synchronize the opposing rhythms, while seamless divisions between the hands are dependent on being over the keys in advance of playing. Clean pedalling, lifting fully at exactly the right moment, will ensure that the texture does not become muddled in the middle section. Here the LH 5ths and octaves which rise by a minor 3rd can be practised as block shapes and agile thumb movement will prevent unevenness in the RH scale figures.

Thinking in long sweeping phrases will capture the horizontal flow of the outer sections. Subtle surges in tone, always with the LH a notch quieter than the melody, contribute to the fleeting character, while incisive staccato and firm rhythm will make the most of the abrupt endings. Lightness and delicacy, avoiding undue accentuation, convey the airy mood midway. In this section, subtle yet distinguishable contrasts between *mp* and *mf* add interest and a well-graded diminuendo and *rit.* will allow the music to evaporate, illusion-like, before the return to D minor.

C:4 Mike Cornick Modulations (TB)

The cool, relaxed style of this piece, with its easy-going rhythms and 'bluesy' 7th harmonies, provides a welcome change from the more classical idioms. Although the music is firmly rooted in the jazz tradition, many skills developed in classical training will be called into play to produce a convincing, expressive performance. A jazz player's unerring sense of pulse is needed for success, as is the impression of total freedom and spontaneity. Time should appear to stand still as the phrases unfold gently within a subtle dynamic range, which never becomes over-robust.

Some initial practice in strict time, feeling a clear crotchet beat, is a good starting point, perhaps omitting ties to help judge the juxtaposition between swung quavers and triplets. Thereafter, however, rhythms should flow flexibly as if improvised. The two-part texture in the RH needs careful fingering to enable notes to be held for their full length. In addition to the marked pedalling at the ending, judicious use elsewhere, using the ear as a guide for clarity in the melodic line, will sustain harmonies.

Your student might imagine the seamlessly legato lines played on the saxophone, with the grace notes, placed slightly before the beat, perhaps evoking slides up to the main note. Playing the chords without the melodic line is an excellent way to appreciate the subtleties of the progressions. The frequent shifts in tonality lead the ear onwards in unexpected ways, and inflections in phrase shape reflect the melodic contours. Occasional accents and staccato details serve to highlight moments along the way, and the improvisatory flourish underlines the calm, dreamy mood of the final bar.

C:5 | Dello Joio Moderate

Here is a hidden gem with a heady mixture of rich textures and blues-inspired harmonies by a relatively unfamiliar Italian-American composer. The piece packs plenty into relatively few bars, creating a languid, peaceful mood through expansive phrasing and expressive 'vocal' lines. Changes of time signature create a quasi-improvisatory freedom, with bar-lines seeming almost irrelevant at times.

Although the relaxed tempo allows room for locating notes comfortably, LH quavers need careful fingering to ensure a smooth line. The upper note of larger stretches may be omitted or redistributed to the other hand, and a tangle will be prevented by keeping the right wrist raised at bars 14–17. Considerable rhythmic ebb and flow suits the style, but ties and double-dotted figures need a firm sense of pulse. The pedal plays a vital part through-out in creating harmonic warmth. The maxim 'pedal with the ears' applies here, with experimentation and critical listening the best guide to frequency of change.

Harmonies based on a 4th create an austerity to the opening, after which the mood gives way to Romantic warmth. A prominent tenor 'voice' emerges from the texture at bar 3, after which the melody soars and dips. Tenuto marks in bar 8 perhaps imply a slight lingering, as if to enjoy the view from the top of a mountain, and rests allow air into the texture at times. Warmer tone enriches the baritone register at the restatement of the melody at bar 14. Your student may like to explore holding the pedal through bars 23–4 to create a dreamlike effect, changing at the final bar to reveal a clear E♭ major harmony.

C:6 | Khachaturian Study

Perhaps this piece with its busy quaver movement and vivid contrasts deserves a more imaginative title than 'Study'. Although it displays neatness and technical facility, colourful harmonic shifts and a wide dynamic palette ensure that musical interest is sustained through to the triumphant C major finish. Quaver patterns are almost constant throughout, with no large stretches, and there are contrasted rhythmic patterns and ideas, including two brief suggestions of a rumba.

Staccato, for which some initial practice using scales or five-finger exercises might be beneficial, is one of the chief technical challenges. A finger touch, keeping close to the keys, will create the clarity and delicacy for the quiet sections, whereas louder outbursts need additional weight from the hand. Initial legato practice might help to cement into memory the unpredictable LH patterns at bars 16–19 and 67–71, the quaver patterns between the hands requiring a percussionist's precision. The descending minim and crotchet patterns (from bars 9 and 30 respectively) may be slurred in pairs, while the other hand maintains the staccato; and shifting between the black keys for the repeated Fs in bars 39–49 will prevent the hands from colliding.

The moderato element of the tempo indication should be taken into account when choosing the optimum, sustainable pace for clarity and precision; the minim feel to the pulse allows the music to travel easily. A wide dynamic range is dependent largely on a *p* that is sufficiently delicate, dropping back at each *a tempo* and saving the *ff* for the two marked areas. Pedal might be extended to the final five bars, and the accents need plenty of attack.

GRADE 7

A:1 **Clementi** Allegro assai (MT)

🎵 The usually sunny disposition of this piece renders it an ideal movement to conclude this charming early Classical sonata. The style of the young Clementi is eclectic here, straddling Mozart and even Scarlatti. Beethoven's shadow lingers too, partly in the richer piano textures, but also in the many adventurous *p*/*f* juxtapositions which populate the section in G minor beginning at bar 83.

✋ This sonata is an excellent choice for students with smaller hands, as it makes bountiful use of 3rds, scalic runs and Alberti-bass accompaniments; the only continuous octaves are the passages of LH semiquavers at bars 45–52 and 98–106, which might conceivably be assisted by deft touches of pedal. Turns and grace notes positioned on the beat should alleviate rhythmic complications. Balance between the hands is an aspect easily overlooked in favour of which hand happens to be busiest! 'Tune is king' would be a sensible way of gauging what deserves promotion throughout, and students should target brilliance in the demisemiquaver flourishes. The Alberti-bass patterns in the LH fall delightfully under the fingers, though the markedly heavier touch of the modern piano can make these notes appear unduly turgid and heavy-going – your student should think more in terms of ballet shoes than wellingtons.

🎨 As with all Classical pieces, attention to articulation is paramount, in particular 'sighs', which serve to round off phrases elegantly; the first example is the B–A quaver couplet in bar 24. The repeated chords at cadences (e.g. at bars 19–20 and 81–2) perhaps invite a hint of a crescendo going forwards in order to avoid stodgy uniformity. The G minor section, a sort of 'development' in sonata-form terminology, invites something altogether new and enterprising, though this should not bring about an unwarranted sagging of tempo. Finally, the restatements of the melodic fragments can always enjoy moments of individuality, as befits all rondo movements.

A:2 **Haydn** Presto (MT)

🎵 Nestled between the composer's earlier, stormier keyboard works and his more transparently Classical later sonatas lies this marvellous example for clavicembalo (harpsichord). Its concluding Presto movement, which follows a familiar monothematic structure, is a pure delight to play. Students wondering how humour finds its way into Haydn's writing need look no further than the passage beginning at bar 33. And yet the development section seems to frown more sternly, building as it does from a diminished 7th chord – a cornerstone of dramatic harmonic writing throughout the eighteenth century.

🖐 On any period instrument the *f* semiquaver patterns at bars 28 and 123 would seem a breeze, whereas tension is a potential hazard for players on a modern piano. The secret is not to bear down from the upper body, but to enjoy the music's oratorical value by gauging a subtle crescendo and ensuring supple, curved fingers. At the development the LH receives first bite at the melody (bar 62); here, and at bars 86–9, avoiding unnecessary jerkiness of the LH – what was once known as a 'quiet' hand – will encourage a smoother delivery. Once coordination has been ironed out at bars 104–11 this passage has the potential to become a favourite.

🎨 From bar 32 onwards Haydn's dynamic palette widens impressively, so that instances of *pp* to *f* become increasingly hard to keep track of. It may be wise to negotiate one or two musical high-points with your students so that an overview emerges sturdily. For a performance to have a gracefulness at the start, the tempo is best moderated to keep within a palpable $\frac{2}{4}$; taken too slickly, it starts to sound as one-in-a-bar, which will doubtless wreak havoc at every turn. Haydn's music often benefits from occasional moments of space between musical gestures (bar 135 presents one such possibility), and once again these are best decided in advance to maximize their impact.

[A:3] D. Scarlatti Sonata in B minor (MT)

🔩 Domenico Scarlatti's fascination for the compact harpsichord sonata (he wrote in excess of 500) seems uncannily parallel to Vivaldi's penchant for the concerto (*c*.500). The ingenuity of both composers ostensibly lies in the realm of instrumental techniques, textures and harmonies; in Scarlatti's case, many twists and turns also await discovery in his melodic guile, spicy ornamentation and his intrepid foreshadowing of sonata form.

🖐 While the term 'Allegrissimo' may cause momentary consternation, the metronome suggestion of ♩ = *c*.104 should counter any notions of unbridled velocity. If a performance attains momentum it is fast enough, especially given the propensity to nudge forward during the passages at bars 24–32 and 55–75. Performances should sparkle and fizz with energy, but evenness is critical; the leaner, scalic flourishes need wrists of rubber and fingers of steel. Articulating the LH quaver lines, which predominate in the sonata, could work with smooth notes or detached notes, or even a mixture, though perhaps the local context should determine the strategy – hence bars 11, 39 and 46 might invite a more emphatic pronouncement to assist cadences. The suggested ornament realizations provided at bars 14, 33 and 39 are eminently pianistic; any deviations from these must always decorate, not contaminate, Scarlatti's immaculately conceived lines.

🎨 Consistency of approach will help students to feel in charge when building their interpretations. Although restraint is the watchword here, the modern piano's special qualities may be allowed to contribute to positive effect, albeit in deference to the intimate beauty of the harpsichord (some larger examples of which had two manuals). For a performance to be communicative it needs inflection and creativity; this should spark invaluable discussion in lessons – whether, for example, to employ echo effects in places such as bars 34–8. The syncopations, which announce important cadences in both halves of the sonata, became firm features during the galant period and present opportunities to inject a little charisma.

A:4　J. S. Bach　Fugue in C　　ⓉⒷ

With its clear-cut textures in a mixture of two and three parts, Bach's Fugue in C is an excellent introduction to fugal writing. Although some students may be deterred by its busy appearance on the page, a player with the discipline and patience to sort out its tricky corners will reap the rewards of this wonderful music. The constant semiquaver movement and cheerful C major tonality contribute to its jaunty character, and the absence of any musical instruction provides opportunity for experimenting with contrasts of articulation and dynamics. Bach's original instrumentation is unclear, but imagining the clarity and attack of the harpsichord is a good starting point.

Maintaining fluency, a key requirement for success, is dependent largely on establishing – and sticking to – fingering. A slightly detached, crisp finger action, with particular attention paid to releasing the weaker fourth and fifth fingers efficiently, will give a brilliance of attack to the semiquavers. Sequential patterns are an aid to learning, but slow separate-hands practice will help to clarify the busier moments, especially when semiquavers switch between the hands. Practising in different rhythms (dotted, etc.) can help to iron out unevenness in the figuration, while discrepancies in pace will be revealed by occasional checking with the metronome, at a variety of speeds.

Identifying and playing each voice individually and in various combinations will uncover the linear texture. Imagining the three voices played by a different instrument, perhaps violin, viola and cello, might help to bring the counterpoint to life. Giving prominence to each new voice, keeping the subsidiary parts quieter, announces the fugal exposition at the opening, but thereafter your student must decide the hierarchical importance of the parts: the suspensions in bars 17–18, for instance, are perhaps worthy of prominence over the bass subject. Sequences offer scope for terraced dynamics, and moments of relaxation in tone provide relief – which in turn highlight the climaxes.

A:5　C. F. C. Fasch　Presto　　ⓉⒷ

Fasch's cheerful movement has a carefree charm and elegance which reflects the spirit of the eighteenth century. Although stylistically somewhat akin to the composer's contemporary Haydn in its quick-witted ideas, always with an element of surprise, this relatively unfamiliar work is given individuality by its quirky twists and turns. Bearing in mind the lighter-toned fortepiano, with its five-octave compass, wooden frame and smaller hammers, will help create a clear, transparent tone quality on the modern instrument. Textures are straightforward so the movement should pose few learning problems, apart from a few unexpected corners in the figuration.

An indication of presto often causes candidates to attempt an over-ambitious tempo. Even though a jaunty two-in-a-bar rhythmic feel is needed to lift the music off the page, clarity and evenness in the detail are of paramount importance. Slow practice will expose any blemishes in the semiquavers, ensuring that divisions between the hands are perfectly matched. Flexible thumb movement, preparing in advance of playing, will enable seamless runs, especially in the descending LH scales towards the end of each half. A bright, firm attack is needed to 'point' the LH melodic notes in bars 9–10 and similar, and rotating the hand will facilitate the figuration in bars 79–81.

Understanding the sonata-form structure, with its three main sections, will enable your student to gain an overview of the movement. The almost total lack of dynamic markings gives the opportunity to experiment. The second theme at bar 13 offers scope for a contrast of mood, and a new key for each statement of the opening figure in the development perhaps suggests a different dynamic level. Semiquaver figuration has its own natural shape and inflection, and crisp, light staccatos will provide energy and colour. A sense of gesture and surprise is created by rests at ends of phrases and the pause at bar 40 offers a moment of repose.

[A:6] John Loeillet Giga (TB)

The brilliance of the harpsichord is at the heart of this joyful, energetic dance movement. A wealth of musical ideas and rhythmic energy ensure that interest is maintained throughout. Listening to the harpsichord's sound, or, better still, playing the instrument, will give an impression of the attack and immediacy of tone required. Variety and character can be provided by the many possible contrasting articulation choices, while the absence of dynamic markings in the score presents a blank canvas for your student's imagination. An understanding of binary structure, with its sense of motion towards the relative major midway before returning to the home key via a series of modulations, will create a framework on which to build a performance.

To find a sustainable tempo, students would be advised to work out their optimum speed for bars 30–35, probably the trickiest section. In these bars, accenting each group's first quaver will help keep the hands safely together; the LH figures may need separate practice. Ornaments, integral to the style, must not disturb the basic four-in-a-bar pulse. Synchronization with the LH needs care, and the rhythm of the inverted mordents may be modified to two semiquavers followed by a quaver for a more comfortable realization.

While a predominantly detached touch suits the quaver figuration, slurring the first two notes of each group in the string-like repeated patterns in bars 16–18 might be explored. The LH plays an important part in providing bounce and airiness to the dance-like rhythms, with ties creating contrast with the otherwise separated chords. A keen ear will make sure that it supports, without overpowering, the main melodic interest. Dynamic inflection, often determined by rise and fall in pitch, should remain within the context of the harpsichord. Sequences offer scope for terraced dynamics (e.g. in bars 35–9), and repetitions of phrases suggest a change of dynamic level, as if switching harpsichord manual.

B:1 **Chopin** Nocturne in C sharp minor

Chopin's supreme gift of melody is showcased in this beautiful piece. After a solemn introduction, the alternating major/minor tonality and *con forza* outbursts of the outer sections create melancholy and passion in equal measure, while a somewhat more pastoral feel characterizes the middle part. The reprise is decorated with rapid and expressive figuration so typical of the composer and at the end all the angst of the night subsides into a peaceful sleep with a final shift to the tonic major.

Balance between melody and accompaniment is crucial and the RH will need weight in the touch to produce a sonorous, rounded sound. Encourage your student to work at the LH part on its own, developing flexible and smooth lateral movement to join the notes as closely as possible. Fingering options for the RH 6ths will be governed in part by hand size. Clarity and evenness in the trills should not be compromised for the sake of speed, and when preceded by the same grace note, as in bar 9, they should begin on the upper note.

A wide dynamic range and expressive shaping within phrases are required to convey the breadth of emotion, and the RH's declamatory style in places such as bars 13 and 46 can have stresses on individual notes within the legato context. Pedal is needed almost throughout, with changes on the first and third beats often being sufficient, but your student should be alert to places where harmonic or textural considerations require something different, such as in bar 17 and throughout the $\frac{3}{4}$ section. Traditionally, this part is often speeded up in performance and this could be tried while observing the subsequent rall. and adagio. Rubato should be sensitively and sparingly used, but reductions of pace, especially in bar 56, may be necessary in order to avoid rushing the delicate scales near the end.

B:2 | Wanghua Chu Love Song

This melody is a traditional folksong from Kangding in the Sichuan province of China. It tells of the mountainside town bathed in moonlight and of the courtship between the woodcutter's daughter and the blacksmith's son. In this arrangement the composer fuses the pentatonic scale and the open 4ths and 5ths so characteristic of Chinese musical idiom with textures and harmonies in the Romantic style. The result is an expressive and evocative piece which feels like an appreciation of a beautiful scene as well as the story of a romance, the melody rising and falling over a gently pulsating syncopation in the bass.

Small hands might struggle a little with the extensive use of chords in the RH and the need to sustain the smoothest possible legato, but the piece will be accessible for most students. Much useful work could be done hands-separately, concentrating on closely connecting the chords, keeping the hand relaxed in an octave stretch and voicing the top notes. In the LH syncopation, choice of fingering on the third and sixth notes of each bar is critical in enabling ease of passage up and down the keyboard. The pedal should be extensively used for the creation of colour and atmosphere, as well as to sustain harmonies; harmonic changes are key to identifying pedal changing points, which are often, though by no means always, every half bar.

Degrees of shape in the phrases, lengths of pauses, amounts of slowing into the pauses, and dynamics beyond those indicated are all areas for your student to explore and make personal interpretative choices about. The bass may be kept a little in the background in the first half, but counter-interest can be created in the more elaborate repeat. The sumptuous chords in bars 31–4 should be powerfully passionate but never harsh in tone, and the lingering close clear but as quiet as possible as we contemplate the moonlit scene.

B:3 | Backer Grøndahl Sommervise (Summer Song)

This lovely character piece has a simple structure and melodic design, but contains a wealth of interesting detail. Its slow-moving phrases and brevity perhaps evoke aspects of the Scandinavian summer – the days are long but the season all too brief. The initial statements of the motifs are graceful yet reserved as the tonality oscillates between major and minor, but in the repeats the atmosphere is warmed with thicker texture and there is a Chopinesque quality to the decorative RH figures. A brief coda drifts through C major and minor before reaching the home key. The pace is unhurried but the music must flow with lilt in the rhythm.

There are considerable technical challenges despite the slow tempo. The double notes must be even and smooth and practice of them could include working in dotted rhythms. All lie well under the fingers, though, with only bar 26 perhaps proving a little awkward for small hands. Another difficulty lies in avoiding bumpy melodic lines when the tune transfers to the LH. Students must make judicious fingering choices, while aiming for the smoothest possible legato, and top notes in the chords will benefit from voicing, with the weight of the hand leaning towards the thumb.

Some pedalling is marked and there is scope for further use, but undue blurring of harmonies and texture should be avoided. In the spread chords of the melody, which is always cantabile, the top note should be timed to coincide with both the other hand and the quaver pulse (e.g. in bar 12). Much of the piece is fairly quiet but the phrases need gentle rise and fall within them, and your student can make the most of the rather more assertive *mf* passage. Using the *una corda* pedal in the last four bars will create colour and atmosphere as the music slows and dies away; perhaps the summer is already only a memory.

B:4 A. Beach Scottish Legend (NO)

Amy Marcy Beach, a significant figure in American music, toured Europe extensively as a pianist and perhaps found her inspiration for 'Scottish Legend' during those travels. While influences of Brahms and Rachmaninov are identifiable, Beach's music here is original and distinctive. The characterful 'Scotch snap' (♪♩.) frequently appears, but this is a more general evocation of a legend. A sense of scale and space is created, with the melody spanning at least an octave in most phrases, and chords over extended intervals suggest a wide vista. A wealth of performance directions invites your student to tell a compelling tale.

Significant challenges arise, notwithstanding the slow tempo. Larger hands have an advantage but flexibility and suppleness are more important. Painstaking work will be needed to avoid bumpy articulation, with numerous fingering options to consider. Pedalling is indicated throughout, for which fingers and foot should be carefully coordinated. However, initial practice without pedal would be a good discipline, and this emphasizes the pedal's use as a source of colour and texture rather than to cover gaps! The appearances of staccato are brief but significant. Touch and tonal range are all-important, with everything from a full-bodied *ff* to the hush of *ppp* required.

Opportunities abound for personalized interpretation and detail. Variation in the execution of pauses, accents and spread chords will avoid repetitiveness, and even the ♪♩ rhythm might be subtly altered, edging towards double-dotted in the more animated D major section. Use of rubato would be an interesting topic for your musically maturing student to explore, and the *sempre cantabile* at the start is a reminder to project the melodic notes consistently. There are some exquisite details to savour, particularly the sudden return to the lament in bar 28 immediately after the passionate climax and the poignant B♭ minor chord in bar 33 as the piece heads towards its whispered close.

B:5 Poulenc Nocturne No. 8

This last of eight Nocturnes, which acts as the coda of the cycle, has a melody similar to that of the first, although all were written separately over the course of a decade. The piece is short and simply structured, and yet Poulenc's melodic invention, distinctive harmonic language, and mastery of texture and range on the keyboard make for deeply expressive and reflective music. Lyricism and beautiful sound are its hallmarks, and playing the top line by itself, noting the varied intervals and keys, would be a good introduction to the composer's individual style.

'Very moderate' is the tempo direction, but considerable challenges are presented in the extensive chordal writing. Separate-hands practice in short sections will be useful, striving to join the chords as smoothly as possible. The melodic line should dominate within the texture throughout; encourage your student to work at this aspect from the start, with the weight leaning towards the outside of the RH, and to find creative fingerings to maintain the legato. Pedal use will be continuous, its changing-points governed by shifts in harmony and also the tune when it moves chromatically, such as in bar 17. Exact coordination between depressing the keys and lifting the foot will avoid bumps and gaps in the lines.

Most of the phrases span four bars, with a little breath midway through each. Attention can be drawn to these shapes, and extra space allowed at the commas. The pace can gradually relax towards the close; elsewhere the music needs to keep moving but there is plenty of scope for rubato. Time can be taken to accommodate the graceful arpeggio in bar 27 and any awkward stretches (e.g. those in bars 19 and 20). The dynamic range is wide, including a sonorous and passionate *f* at bar 18, and the bare 5ths at the end (recalling the key of the first Nocturne) need a hushed and luminous quality.

B:6 Schubert *Moments musicaux* No. 1

The *Moments musicaux*, like the Impromptus, are among Schubert's best loved and most widely performed works for piano, and this, the first of the set, is a delightful character piece. Written in ternary form, the whimsical and imaginative outer sections have variations in metre, articulation and mood which give them an improvisatory quality. In between, a beautiful melody glides above a rich texture, telling a heartfelt and expressive story. Passion, wonder and sorrow are all present before harmonic suspensions over a pedal

G herald the return to the opening phrase. Schubert's fusion of Classical and Romantic styles is vividly apparent.

The variety and control of articulation needed is perfectly illustrated in the first eight bars. A quick silent change of fingers on the dotted quaver in bar 1 will enable a smooth legato and the subsequent staccato chords need positive attack. Accurate assimilation of details where the rhythm and articulation differ between the hands, such as bars 10–12, is vital and separate-hands practice will help. Where a student's stretch cannot accommodate the chords, timing the top note to coincide with the other hand and the beat, such as in bars 28 and 49, is a good general rule, and there are a few places where playing adjacent white notes with the thumb works well.

The tempo is not fast, but the phrases must flow and students may explore the use of rubato – nothing extreme, but plenty of ebb and flow within the musical sentences. The pace may be eased before the pause at the lovely conclusion to the middle section. A wide dynamic range is called for, and the insistent rhythms and chords in bars 13–16 can get quite stormy while the D major section from bar 38 is utterly serene (care should be taken to avoid an overly intrusive bass part here). Melodies invite projection with cantabile tone, and the silent bars need their full three beats to achieve the desired dramatic effect.

C:1 | Ravel Valse (Waltz)

The tradition of writing groups of waltzes for piano, which was given such originality by Schubert, encouraged later composers to follow suit. Schubert's two sets, *Valses sentimentales* and *Valses nobles*, directly inspired Ravel's similarly named set (from which this piece is taken) and would make an enjoyable starting point for study. Ravel composed several fine pieces based on the waltz, including the orchestral masterpiece *La Valse*, where the tradition was pushed almost to stylistic breaking point. Further ideas to help with Ravel's tonal palette might be found in the subtle play of light and colour in Monet's paintings, which contrast with the bolder brushstrokes and vivid colours of Van Gogh, for example.

Here it is apparent that the Classical/Romantic harmonies of Schubert have been left far behind. Hours of fascination for your student lie ahead, discovering how the sea of accidentals floating across the notes fit together to create dissonance, consonance and a unique harmonic language. Where the LH crosses over the RH to pick out bell-like dotted crotchets (bars 19–20, 23–4) the desired control of tone and texture may need patient practice. Suitable tonal transparency overall will benefit from a pliable finger touch and loose wrist; the dissonances should be persuasive and piquant, rather than spiky. The bass notes provide an important foundation for the upper lines to flow across; some of these have tenuto marks, but all need resonance and a sense of direction.

Ravel has added many directions on the score; each one is as essential as the notes. He has not indicated rubato and the music's delicate momentum needs only very subtle touches, if any. Sensitivity to harmonic nuance and the almost intangible 'wisp of wind' texture can create a compelling interpretation. Effective communication is not easily guaranteed, but it is much more likely from a musician alert to the music's beauties, and with the imagination to become absorbed in the waft and whirl of this dreamy dance.

C:2 Christopher Norton Forcing the Pace

By this grade, pianists who seek out the jazzy options in exams will be familiar with Norton's attractive style. Although popular worldwide for his piano music, he has also composed ballet scores and musicals, so students might like to expand their enjoyment by tracking down his recent micro-musical *The Vikings*, for example, or his beautiful Clarinet Sonata. For those new to playing rock-style music, listening to Led Zeppelin's songs will get the foot tapping and switch on the magic of irrepressible syncopation.

A helpful comment about the Prelude's structure is included in the footnote. The metronome marking is extremely fast and a slightly slower alternative has been suggested for exam use. However, wise preparation of this piece will ignore both, in the early stages; familiarity with the notes' geography and the development of a rich, vibrant tone will benefit from a more leisurely approach. Top speeds will come easily enough when accurate foundations have been laid and all musical details understood. Norton's use of slurs, staccato dots and accents is very precise and is geared to help students acquire a stylish 'rock' rhythm, so this patience will be well-rewarded. His dynamic scheme creates a satisfying musical structure and pedal indications are often specific. However, there is no reason why your students should not add to the dynamic and pedal markings, according to their own imagination and spur-of-the-moment ideas.

With notes, rhythms and shaping in place, the player is ready to unroll the requested vigour. The syncopations, if accurately controlled in practice, come to life at faster tempos and a sensation of springing from one to another should be addictively exciting. At this point, confident resonance can enhance the bigger moments; performance enthusiasm may blossom into complete abandon within the sounds being drawn from the piano. Such engagement is very infectious; listeners (including the examiner!) will enjoy being swept along by the ever-increasing energy.

⬚C:3⬚ **Absil** Humoresque

This is music of energy and sparkle, spiced with a considerable sense of humour. Very little of it is quiet, but the texture is lean, with two-part writing, and some unison, across much of it. As if to compensate, the music often appears to be in two keys at once, and the rhythms contradict the $\frac{2}{4}$ time signature in a teasing manner. 'Humoresque' would be an excellent choice for a pianist with small hands, for nimbleness and a lively sense of rhythm and fun are the important requirements for success here.

Strict rhythmic control and very even semiquavers will be needed as a foil for the unexpected timbres of the syncopated clashes. Chromatic runs should, by this stage, fall under the fingers with ease, but their rapidity here may benefit from preparatory work: slow practice, with fingertips as close to the keys as possible; the use of different rhythmic patterns, so as to uncover slight unevenness of thumb movement. Neatness in the LH staccato bars can be secured by practising at different speeds, but always with the hand kept still and staccatos achieved by finger movement alone. All these three practice methods can help with the coordination required in bars 11–14. Metronome work might assist as the slower tempos are gradually brought up to *Molto vivo*.

Consideration might be given to whether all accented notes should have equal weight. A sense of slight growth in intensity could build up their insistency and avoid a repetitive effect.

Familiarity with the harmonic colour of the offbeat chords in the middle section can be helped by slow, listening exploration. Your student might compare how the arrangement of major and minor intervals differs, giving a more or less dissonant spikiness in each. This could be further explored by playing the chords at the treble or bass ends of the keyboard, to hear how extremes of pitch affect their resonance.

⬚C:4⬚ **Brian Bonsor** Willie Wagglestick's Walkabout

For pianists who have enjoyed playing boogie before, this ebullient and extrovert piece is a chance to let their hair down. Those who are experimenting with jazz for the first time might listen to Oscar Peterson playing 'Boogie Blues Etude' or 'Honky Tonk Train Blues', which will show how much fun can be had performing in this style.

Your student may be perplexed by a few features on the score: boogie tremolos are places for a really abandoned sense of showmanship, with the bars needing to last their full time, but not requiring any particular precision in rhythm or tone. Placing the hands over the chords, much like a large wild bear, and giving them a good shake into the keys will achieve the most satisfying rumble. (It's worth noting here that the tremolo Bs in bars 33 and crotchet Bs in bar 35 are B♮s, giving a bright major 7th chord; B♭s, a softer effect, have been wrongly printed in the past.) The two-against-three rhythms of bars 21–3 may have already been mastered but, if still giving trouble, the words 'hot chocolate' spoken twice in each bar to a ♩ ♫ ♩ pattern could help the combined rhythm of the hands feel more natural.

Bars 21–3 additionally include plenty of articulation detail and, as elsewhere in the piece, these seemingly inconspicuous markings are important in giving rhythmic vitality. However, a really convincing performance will discover much more shape, detail and tonal variety than is printed. Entering fully into the spirit of this music, leaving any inhibitions or shyness resolutely outside the exam-room door, is the key to a successfully communicative performance. The examiner will thoroughly enjoy a laid-back and imaginatively coloured romp and his or her foot may well be tapping by the time of the completely casual, final deep C.

C:5 Dello Joio Bright

This Italian American composer formed his own jazz band at the age of 20 and went on to study composition at New York's Juilliard School. Despite his love of jazz, there is little evidence of it in the Suite (1940), from which this lively piece is the very short second movement. Its false relations between sharp, natural and flat, and the many offbeat chords or accents, do however recall jazz sounds popular at the time. Intervals of a 4th and a 5th feature frequently in the music, giving an outdoorsy and typically American timbre.

Rhythmically and melodically, much is made of a limited number of note patterns. This means that learning of the notes should be relatively quick. However, a few awkward leaps and widely spread chords will require a good sense of keyboard geography and large or strong hands. When practising the rapid RH shifts along the keyboard in the opening bars, students need to maintain as much relaxation in arm and wrist as possible, so that performances avoid tension creeping into the whole piece. Especially tricky are the semiquaver chords in bar 12, which are fast at this bright tempo. It will be important to begin learning them slowly and perhaps gently, so that they remain relaxed in performance.

Markings for slur, staccato, accent and tenuto are carefully printed and sometimes combined, in order to convey exactly the sonority needed. In addition, rhythms can gain vitality if strong and weak beats have a slightly different weight. The sparkling semiquavers of the opening bars might also be given detailed light and shade, according to their position in each beat. Gradations of tone will help sculpt the phrases; in this piece, decrescendos can be especially effective in providing contrast to the energy found elsewhere. With all these essential details fully absorbed, the music needs only to gain a sense of excitement and enjoyment for the performance to convince and delight.

 **Dave Grusin** Ray's Blues

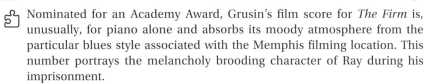 Nominated for an Academy Award, Grusin's film score for *The Firm* is, unusually, for piano alone and absorbs its moody atmosphere from the particular blues style associated with the Memphis filming location. This number portrays the melancholy brooding character of Ray during his imprisonment.

A relaxed tempo helps develop this mood and allows semiquavers to find stylish rhythmic inequality. They need a slightly long/short unevenness, but the underlying beats should maintain a steady pulse. These runs might find a suitably hazy sound if the fingers are held a little flatter than in classical piano music, with loose wrists and fingering shifts sometimes brushing the keys with the back of the fingers, rather than the more conventional passing of thumb underneath. For example, the first set of semiquavers might place finger 2 on all the notes that are sharpened, with thumb only used for the first note. This scheme helps to establish a fluid rhythmic unevenness, as well as a very slight emphasis on the 'blue' notes. A similar approach for the lazily eloquent quaver 'break' near the end, with hand held almost like a bunch of bananas, should give the player a chance to traverse its awkward angles with freedom of movement and expressive shape.

Pedal could be used almost throughout and a careful ear will judge how and when to change, according to the performance piano and room. Ray's desperation can be expressed by highlighting the more dissonant chords or notes, especially those that arrive off the beat. Marvellous tonal colouring is possible on any number of the harmonies that Grusin lands on, and an ability to play very softly, or warmly, or with focus on special notes within the most mysterious chords, would lend the performance persuasive conviction. Above all, a sense of identification with the man's feelings can be communicated in a powerful way, if the pianist is truly listening to the sounds coming from the instrument.

GRADE 8

A:1 **J. S. Bach** Gigue

This is a perfect fugue wrapped up in a rollicking dance. Bach's Orchestral Suite No. 4 contains a similar gigue fugue within its overture, and the timbres of oboes, trumpets and strings lend a cheerful brightness there. It might make inspiring listening, promoting ideas about stylish articulation and suitably colourful dynamic range; a recent recording on Baroque instruments would be ideal.

The score contains editorial fingering suggestions; these work well, but are not the only options. A reliable fingering scheme tends to be essential for security; schemes that vary on each playing are likely to cause stumbles when it matters most, even if they appear fine in relaxed practice. Fingering planning can help to ensure that long notes remain sustained (e.g. the treble voice, bars 7–9), so that contrapuntal lines are intact. Articulation can be chosen to enhance the dance quality and encourage one-in-a-bar flow. Slurs might be distributed (over two notes or three) to mark each half-bar, with intervening notes lightly detached. A legato approach is also possible, but touches of articulation give vitality and are more stylish. Whatever is chosen, the fugue subject should be consistently played throughout the piece. Episodes can give contrast; for example, a more legato touch in semiquavers from mid bar 9 to bar 14, the dance kept buoyant with gentle staccatos on second- and fourth-beat LH quavers.

The music's overall structure would benefit from slight breaths before subject entries mid bar 14 and at the end of bar 43. The Gigue's possible climax, around bar 52, can have the loudest dynamic, but perhaps f rather than ff. One or two favourite lyrical moments may take the softest level that can safely be controlled; this might need checking in the try-out of the exam piano. Dynamic shading between these levels can be explored elsewhere, according to taste. Very little pedal is needed, although subtle touches might occasionally add colour in episodes and as the glorious end is reached.

A:2 **Handel** Fugue in B flat

Handel's large-scale choral fugues, from *Messiah* and other oratorios or anthems, are so popular that it is a treat for pianists to encounter one of his six rarely played keyboard fugues. Their invention is considerable and they make effective concert pieces. This particular one is noble in character, but lively, with sunny chains of parallel 3rds or 6ths and suspensions – all the ingredients of an irresistible Baroque brew!

The suggested fingerings assist in ensuring accurate voice-leading, especially the many finger substitutions. The middle voice jumps between the hands occasionally; matching of tone across these points needs attentive listening. Subject and counter subject both contain elements that could be either detached or more cantabile. Choice of articulation can vary, but preferences established in the exposition should be consistently reproduced wherever matching patterns recur. An effective point of articulation is to detach notes that spring up a 4th onto a tied note, for example the treble voice in bar 2. Discovering the many places where this occurs, sometimes in two voices at once, helps bring rhythmic vitality and contrapuntal clarity. The ensuing tied notes often launch sequences of suspensions; these should be played legato and become softer as dissonance resolves to consonance.

Performances of this fugue will best take flight when a confidently firm but singing tone has been achieved and the tempo can support energy and momentum. Pedal will hardly be needed in this busy writing, but may add warmth at the close. Despite the lack of printed directions, phrase shaping and dynamic interest are key to a successful interpretation. Good moments for softer levels might be the modulation to G minor in bars 23–5 and the episode at bars 44–6. Between these, a build-up to the D minor cadence in bars 43–4 would enhance the structure. Similar variety can be found in the remaining sections, but always with an ear for texture and harmonic progress towards the richly grand finish.

A:3   R. K. Shchedrin   Prelude and Fugue in A minor

This would make an adventurous and rewarding choice for your students, as well as their listeners. In a long historical line of homages to Bach's genius in counterpoint, Shchedrin's contribution combines ingenious flair for the 'old style' with exciting new sounds. The Prelude fizzes and sparkles, with cross-rhythms refracting the patterns. The Fugue's harmonies are undeniably gritty, but the clashes work powerfully in propelling the music forwards and periodic pauses highlight vibrantly intriguing chords.

Agility and light precision are needed in the Prelude; its technical challenges include some awkward broken-chord patterns (e.g. bars 25–9 in the RH), where a flexible lateral turning of the wrist may help negotiate the shifts. The tricky repeated notes in bars 41–4 will become much easier when mentally grouped to point up the phrase shapes: between the third and fourth semi-quavers of each bar, the phrase changes direction.

The Fugue's complexity might be well-served by a slightly slower tempo than the one suggested. Fingering patterns which ensure consistent joining of notes, wherever possible, will give the best results. Pedal use may suit the broad expressive quality of this very chromatic music, but frequent and neat changes will be needed to maintain clarity of texture. Crotchet-beat changing is often appropriate, but some pairs of quavers may need individual touches (e.g. bar 11, beat 3). The extended pedal indication at bars 42–4 suggests that longer pedalling may suit where the main activity is repeated crotchets, for example in bars 1, 4 and 55.

Jewel-like in its brilliance and concentration, the Prelude evaporates as mysteriously as it arrived. The brooding atmosphere of the Fugue, with expressively angular interval shapes and resonant bass notes, immediately catches the attention. A really effective interpretation will need to be thoroughly familiar with the contrapuntal and structural workings, as explained in the note below the title. If they can be given coherence and shape, so that listeners grasp the musical argument, Shchedrin's two-part piece will make a memorable experience.

[A:4] J. S. Bach Prelude and Fugue in D minor (MMM)

The Preludes and Fugues of *Das wohltemperirte Clavier* are one of the foundations of the keyboard player's repertoire, so if you are looking for an alternative List A piece, this may well fit the bill. The Prelude is among Bach's most exciting and the Fugue not unduly taxing once some initial study has been done.

Agile fingers will be essential for the Prelude, with an equal demand placed on both hands. Separate-hands practice will help to build independence once suitable fingerings have been decided. The ability to move the hand smoothly over the keys when the fifth finger or thumb is required to play black keys will be important. The attack is brilliant, but there should also be quieter moments to add colour. For instance, a diminuendo starting in bar 14 could lead to *p* for the murmuring figure in bars 18–21, and the same figure, from bar 57, suggests a relatively quiet ending.

The shape of the Fugue's subject is easily seen. Whirling triplets rise upwards to the top before the melody falls back, chromatically at first, in quavers. In bar 3 the treble voice answers in the dominant, and halfway through this bar the counter subject appears. Care must be taken not to confuse the semiquavers of this theme with the triplets – the pace of the quavers needs always to be kept in mind. After the subject appears in the bass (bars 6 and 7), there are several partial *stretti*, the most interesting at bars 17–18 where the subject is inverted in the middle and bass voices.

Apart from the obvious rise and fall of the subject and counter subject, dynamics are a matter of personal choice. Articulation should be mostly legato, but in the long episode that begins in bar 18 the quavers attached to the triplet groups sound effective if they are detached. The descending semiquavers in bar 24 prepare the way for a strong final statement of the subject.

A:5 | **Hindemith** Interludium and Fuga decima in D flat

Paul Hindemith's landmark work, *Ludus tonalis* (Tone Games), was written in 1942. It consists of a set of 12 fugues connected by 11 interludes, the whole being framed by a prelude and postlude. It is a remarkable composition in which symmetry plays a large part. The postlude is a retrograde inversion of the prelude and the key system, unlike that of Bach's or Shostakovich's, is a cycle of diminishing intervals surrounding C.

At first glance the complex rhythms and plethora of accidentals may seem daunting, but after a closer inspection patterns and sequences begin to emerge. While learning the RH melody of the Interludium, it would be wise to count a slow quaver beat. It is sometimes difficult to cope with finding the notes and learning the rhythm at the same time, so tapping both parts would be helpful. With the LH it is more a question of memorizing the chord shapes, and very often one or two notes are the same in a succession of chords. For instance, in bars 8–10 and 16–18 using fingers 1 and 2 will help to anchor the chords.

Spending some time analysing the Fuga will make it easier for your student to convey the shape and meaning of the music in performance. Finding the subject at bar 1 (middle voice) and 10 (treble), the answer (in the dominant) at bar 3, the third voice at bar 6 (bass) and the two *stretti* between treble and middle voices at bars 12 and 15, will greatly help with interpretation. The first section then closes quietly in bar 18 with all three voices in unison on A♭. Though the second half of the Fuga is notated enharmonically your student should be able to identify the same material unfolding in reverse and in inversion. To round it off, the movement closes with a statement of the subject back in its original form.

A:6 | **Lekeu** Fughetta

The young Belgian composer, Guillaume Lekeu was born in 1870 but died tragically from typhoid at the age of 24. Judging by the 50 works that he had written, and in particular this magnificent Fughetta, his death is a great loss to the music world. He studied with, among others, the great organist and composer César Franck, whose influence can be heard in Lekeu's piano writing. His only piano sonata is in five movements, two of which are fugal, and this Fughetta lies at the heart of the work.

The subject is a four-bar melody in B minor that winds downwards until rising stepwise in the fourth bar. The middle voice answers in the dominant while a counter subject moves sedately underneath. At its subsequent entries the counter subject undergoes considerable alterations. The three voices are often widely spaced, and it is important to notice when the RH must take notes written on the bass stave. As the final climax (bars 52–5) is approached, it would be helpful to slow a little in order to accommodate the spread chord in bar 53. Here your student might prefer to play four of the notes with the LH, leaving just D♯ and A to the RH.

It is organ-like in character, so it would be helpful to imagine the colours of various organ stops, and at the climaxes where octaves are employed the thrilling timbre of the organ pedals can be heard. The pace is unhurried; a speed of ♩ = c.56 will allow the music to unfold majestically. Where the texture is thin with only one or two voices, it is effective to play without any sustaining pedal, but with the entry of the third voice in bar 12 and where the texture becomes more chordal, sustaining pedal will not only assist the legato but add grandeur to the tone. Your student should bear in mind that this is of the late-Romantic sound-world.

A:7 Reicha Fugue No. 1 (MMM)

Described by Beethoven as 'fugues that are not fugues' and by a critic as 'fugalized fantasies', Reicha's set of 36 Fugues was published in 1803. The composer explained that he had evolved a new set of rules for the form, and indeed many of them diverge considerably from the Baroque format. Subjects may appear on any degree of the scale, unusual time signatures like $\frac{12}{4}$ and $\frac{2}{8}$ are used as well as asymmetrical rhythms and polyrhythms. In many ways Reicha was far ahead of his time.

This Fugue, the first of the set, begins quite conventionally. A horn-like figure based on the notes of the tonic triad announces the start of the subject. This is followed by a two-bar pattern of rippling semiquavers played twice. Still in conventional mode, the answer appears in the dominant at bar 7 with the third voice entering in the bass eight bars later. So far so good! Thereafter, the horn figure becomes disconnected from the semiquavers, popping up from time to time in the episodes. The main focus now is on the semiquaver theme and its counter subject that moves in the ♩ ♪ pattern first seen in bars 9–10. The biggest challenge lies with the inner voice trills in bars 60–62. If they are to be attempted, it is advisable to practise them in demisemiquavers with a triplet placed on the fifth note of every LH semiquaver group. Finger substitution will be needed for the sustained notes above.

The composer has provided some dynamic marks, but further ones should be included to colour sequences, and add shape to the phrasing. The build-up to the massive climax begins with a rising chromatic passage in bar 56. A steep crescendo leads to stretto entries of the subject, a burst of LH octaves and some chromatic chords that come to rest on an *ff* diminished 7th chord. With a nod to tradition, the fugue ends quietly with a cadential phrase marked Adagio.

A:8   D. Scarlatti   Sonata in E   (MMM)

 Domenico Scarlatti became master of the court chapel to the King of Portugal in 1719 and was responsible for tutoring the young Princess Maria Barbara. Ten years later she married the heir to the Spanish throne and Scarlatti moved with her to Spain. It is thought by some musicologists that almost all of his 555 or more keyboard sonatas were written for Maria Barbara, and that over half were written during the last six years of his life!

A warm cantabile tone will best suit the Andante passages, but in the brilliant Allegro sections many of the quavers should be staccato. The occasional echo dynamic will add colour – for instance, *f* at bars 36–7 followed by *p* for bars 38–9. When a figure is played three times excitement is created by increasing the volume for each one; bars 76–8 provide a clear example. Something of the fire of Spanish dance can be heard in the section beginning at bar 42 with strumming guitars and stamping feet as the music passes through minor keys. The demisemiquaver figures are written-out ornaments and should be played briskly. Most trills begin on the upper note, but those in bars 73 and 76–8 may be more comfortable played as three-note trills starting on the principal note. The trill in bar 49 is to a D♮.

 The alternating sections of Andante and Allegro afford the player plenty of scope for contrast and changes of mood. The slower sections are full of expressive gestures, especially the falling sequences in bars 11–13 in the first Andante, and the minor tonality of the second. Careful use of pedal will add colour, but should never be allowed to blur the harmony or cover the tiny breaths that occur at many of the bar-lines. Although frequent repetitions invite the use of echo dynamics, this effect should be used sparingly to avoid making it sound fussy.

B:1   **Beethoven**   Rondo   (MT)

Belonging to the composer's early period, the sonata-rondo finale to this splendid work sports an irresistible *joie de vivre*; Beethoven successfully melded Haydn's feisty mood changes (e.g. the B section at bar 21) and Mozart's operatic grandeur (the C section at bar 47). A great deal of the musical material is derived from scales, chromatic scales and arpeggios. The whole is certainly greater than the sum of its parts, however; indeed, the challenge for today's interpreter is to thread these elements together so that they achieve an almost *giocoso* allure.

 There is much to edify the diligent student here. Even the LH's opening triplets present something of a challenge and might best be accomplished by the subtlest emphasis on the first notes to produce a contrary-motion scale effect against the RH. From bar 12 and elsewhere, the semiquaver scales need to glide with an impeccable *legatissimo*, as if passing a baton between the hands, thereby generating a delightful dialogue. The key of E major, with its equitable division of white and black notes, falls comfortably under fingers of different sizes; nevertheless, wandering too far into the black notes should be discouraged, and jerky thumb-passing may be minimized if students memorize short sequences and police their movements themselves.

From its opening bars the music brims with Beethoven's signature devices – the crescendo *p* and offbeat *sf* in bars 3–5, for example. Here, and at reprises, it may be helpful to think of a gavotte, where the music picks up from the bar's second beat, implying a firm arrival (not rude bump) over the bar-line. From bar 47 a melodic line can be picked out if the RH's first notes have an incisive attack; this is best practised as block chords initially, against decisively crisp LH octaves. It may be advisable to take a physical breath just before the A section reprise, at bar 83, if only to ensure a calm, prepared mind.

B:2 Mozart Allegro

Even at the tender age of 19 Mozart's style is strikingly distinctive, consistent and refined. The arpeggiated, 'operatic' RH flourish which launches this first known sonata would become a favourite curtain-raiser of his; indeed, several sonatas begin this way. On a fortepiano speech-like articulation is an inestimably important feature; its leather hammers and lightning-quick action were superbly matched to the composer's boundless imagination for lyrical and dramatic detail. Dynamics would have been perfectly achievable too, though on the modern instrument we need to recalibrate our parameters and seize all chances to tease out the music's elegant turns of phrase.

The LH Alberti-bass accompaniment (bars 5–8 and similar) leaves open the prospect for finger-pedalling, thus permitting the harmonies to 'bloom' more satisfyingly without causing undue blurring to Mozart's fastidious articulation markings. It is surprisingly rare to encounter bars where both hands have semiquaver movement at precisely the same moment – mostly, these occur where the composer either wants extra emphasis, by doubling in the other hand (bar 56), or wishes to showcase areas of increasing intensity (bars 31–4). The cheeky, Haydnesque grace-note passages at bars 26–30 and 87–91 can be practised initially with the two notes sounding together, though they leap more charismatically from the page when played as they appear in the score.

Even in racy Allegro movements, there are isolated opportunities for letting in a little light and shade (e.g. bars 16 and 69), and an ambition overall might be to sound fluid in the more extended running passages, as opposed to overly impulsive or eager. There are regions of volatility to savour too, especially in the development, where daring sequences carry the music from G minor to F major (bars 39–48). Played effectively, the feminine endings (longer, emphasized notes followed by shorter, unstressed notes, such as in bars 5–8) will do much to set up the Viennese sound-world.

B:3 | **Haydn** Presto

The opening movement to this vibrant sonata (composed *c*.1783) forms a cornerstone of Haydn's apotheosis in keyboard writing. In parallel with Mozart, Haydn would spearhead the Viennese style towards unprecedented heights of mastery. The possibilities that the new fortepiano presented for dramatic contrast must have seemed thrilling, and, while hardly evident from the dearth of expressive markings on the autograph manuscript, it is clear that Haydn's reappraisal of texture heralded a new, radical pianistic language.

Despite its innocuous appearance at first sight, this piece is not an easy option. Haydn's technical demands go considerably beyond lengthy running passages: declamatory octaves, orchestrally conceived textures, finger-pedalling, and intrepid leaps in register. Each component needs breaking down into manageable chunks at a more thoughtful pace, though fingerings must also work efficiently up to speed. It is worth seeing where LH and RH fingerings can coincide in the unison runs at bars 27 and 92. The LH F♯ in bar 92 might equally be played with fourth finger, since this encourages third fingers at the start of the next semiquaver figure.

Memorizing the LH octaves (bars 14–15, 51–2) will encourage a cleaner staccato attack and fewer splashes; here, as when this material is in single notes, the wrist may come off the keyboard at the end of each gesture to minimize tension and maximize the sense of moving forward.

Unlike in Haydn's finales, his clever structural gambits here need time to make themselves obvious, so a reckless response to the Presto marking is inadvisable. The few dynamic indications are editorial, presumably reflecting the possibilities for playing on a harpsichord. Choices should be weighed up systematically, but once all surface details have been absorbed a sense of spontaneity and caprice should emerge. Bars 36–41 and 95–108 need careful unpicking to ensure transparency of texture and maintaining of pace; top-note voicing will help make pianistic sense of these deceptively tricky bars.

B:4 | **C. P. E. Bach** Allegro

The most illustrious and celebrated of J. S. Bach's 20 offspring, Carl Philipp Emanuel, helped to establish a new dimension to keyboard writing during the eighteenth century. He was daringly out of kilter with the prevailing galant style, often preferring turbulent, dramatic effects to balanced, neat symmetry. Written while living in Hamburg in the 1770s, this delightful Allegro is the finale to a three-movement sonata, and C. P. E.'s favoured keyboard, the clavichord, is likely the one he had in mind. With the modern piano, players need not be unduly timid with dynamic involvement, nor indeed articulation.

While many of the triplet figures fall tidily under the fingers, muscular memory will benefit from applying a uniform approach to fingering in the sequences wherever possible, as marked – for example, third finger to start bars 8, 10 and 12. Ornaments can, if necessary, be pared down so as not to clutter important rhythmic detail, for, as C. P. E. himself cautioned, ornaments 'are spices which may ruin the best dish'. Your student should guard against startling changes of tempo at bars 25 and 114, where a calmer mood arrives unannounced (though a measured easing off might be appropriate), or conversely, to excessively push on the pace in response to the brilliant, harpsichord-style writing at bars 17, 60 and 106.

Though the musical language of this Classical sonata was freshly innovative for its day, the ability to move at will through myriad keys within a single piece was something made possible by C. P. E.'s father in his 48 Preludes and Fugues, half a century earlier. Expression should therefore be gauged in relation both to the imagined characteristics of the period instruments, and the music's ever-changing moods, or 'affects', as C. P. E. described them. Points of special interest include the fantastical RH tremolo at bars 74–8 and 93–4 – welcome opportunities to bristle with ebullient energy. Opportunities to contrast crescendos with more abrupt dynamic changes should be savoured, and a thought spared for the more intimate regions, too.

B:5 Beethoven Allegro (MT)

Beethoven's first sonata, composed in 1793–5, coincided with the 25-year-old's inaugural public performance in Vienna. The extent to which Beethoven was influenced by Haydn, the sonata's dedicatee, seems debatable; indeed, the 'Mannheim Rocket' arpeggio motif, which launches this racy opening Allegro movement, resonates more with Mozart's style. Beethoven's five-octave wooden-framed fortepiano produced a considerably more intimate sound than today's iron-framed concert grand. Immediacy of attack and rapid note decay were married to the fortepiano's notably lighter action; weighing up such characteristics will help students ensure that dynamic projection and choice of speed are optimally gauged to fit the modern instrument.

Incisiveness of touch, rhythmic drive and secure coordination will contribute to a satisfying account. A supple wrist will permit the LH tremolos to burble away menacingly in bar 20 and elsewhere. The LH is entrusted with important melodic material too (e.g. at bars 9–10 and for several bars from bar 67), but mostly it is tasked with propelling the music forward; the accented off-beat notes, in bars 33–9 for example, deserve special attention. Scalic RH runs that are immaculately honed will be a delight to reel off and will doubtless benefit from thoughtful separate-hands practice.

Features characteristic of Beethoven's music abound, especially the *sf* effects, which lend an engaging, spirited feel to bars 73–80, and the *subito pp* at bar 135. An athletic overall pace, taking account of the ¢, ought not to impede a controlled dispatch of the music's more taxing dramatic gestures.

An overly pecked attack for the opening motif, and for the innumerable wedge staccato markings, may sound rather brittle on the modern piano. Judicious touches of pedal here and there will help to avoid a dry appearance and provide welcome colour. Much excitement can be teased out in the development section, particularly in its *pp* closing stages, bars 93–100, where ideally the pulse should not slacken.

B:6 J. B. Cramer Largo assai–Allegro agitato (MT)

An anglicized German composer and pianist of considerable stature, Cramer ran a successful London music publishing business, which also designed and built high-quality instruments. His technical accomplishments at the keyboard were perhaps more revered than his compositions, and yet Cramer composed around 200 keyboard sonatas, many demonstrating cutting-edge idiomatic writing. Cramer's style resonated with his Viennese contemporaries, particularly Beethoven and Haydn, as well as Field and Dussek, who had arrived from other parts of Europe. The present edition of 2010, by Christopher Hogwood, brings to the music a welcome freshness and does much to redress anomalies and inconsistencies present in earlier editions.

The suspenseful opening takes the guise of an extravagantly textured 16-bar introduction. The rhythm initially sports a double-dotted appearance; nonetheless, do heed the marking Largo assai. From its resplendent, seven-note arpeggiated opening *f* chord the music oozes expressive potential, yet perhaps surprisingly the ensuing Allegro agitato darts off in C minor; in impact, the coupling together of these two sections is perhaps not so far removed from Beethoven's 'Pathètique'. In the Allegro, the LH has some 9th intervals to overcome (bars 43–4 and 47–8), albeit in the context of broken-octave accompaniment; indeed, sustaining this Beethovenian effect without tensing up presents a technical challenge.

Venturesome students should find this a hugely rewarding work, not least for its wide-ranging tonality, temperament and dynamics (*pp* to *ff*). Pedal is indispensable where marked, though perhaps especially at bars 173–6. However, judicious employment is not to be discouraged elsewhere where the textures broaden sufficiently, either to assist the aforementioned majestic chords in the Largo, or to sweeten enigmatic moments in the Allegro, such as bars 28 and 55–62. Elsewhere, the decidedly adventurous harmonic scheme of the music invites careful appraisal, not merely to avoid note misreadings where the key signature changes, but in pursuit of a concrete musical overview.

B:7 Mozart Allegro in B flat (MT)

Mozart penned this Allegro for an incomplete sonata in 1781 while lodging in Vienna. From its opening fanfare-like arpeggiated motif an infectious vivacity springs forth, though at bar 4 the cadence is interrupted, a foreshadowing of the composer's mischievous inclination perhaps. A tempo of ♩ = 112 is more than adequate to impress in the concerto-like flourishes, but will permit some Schubertian lyricism, too; a new theme appears unannounced in the development, apparently to evoke Constanza Weber (later Mozart's wife) and Sophie, her sister.

For the running passages to 'flow like oil' as Mozart envisaged, it is advisable to use strong fingers wherever possible, hence the indicated finger 3s at bar 8, which imply fourth finger on the D♮ and then a deft 3-over-4 movement – a really useful trick which can be employed in wide-ranging repertoire. Something similar may be achievable at bars 37–9; then, at bar 40, placing a fourth finger on the first D then finger 5 on the first B♮ will help minimize jerkiness in the broken octaves. Unison runs, among the trickiest demands a composer can make, are best achieved wrist-free in bars 15, 61 and 105. Your student can tease out the LH 'cello' line at bars 8–12 and 51–8, and allow a little directional crescendo to the octaves, especially those at bars 23–5 and 113–15.

The score contains only the tiniest smattering of dynamic markings, but this shouldn't prevent students from presenting a vivid, characterful performance. Though the default dynamic is *f*, there is scope to be active in phrasing to engage with Mozart's adventurous harmonies. By contrast, articulation markings are plentiful, and it is in this regard that a crystalline, effervescent account is best accomplished. Octave doublings of the melody (bars 44–50 and elsewhere) are to be treasured; the sweetest cantabile here will capture the indicated sighs and bring Mozart's inbuilt contrasts to life.

B:8 H. O. C. Zinck Allegro con brio

Under the tutelage of C. P. E. Bach, Hardenack Zinck (a German-Danish composer and choral trainer) settled first in Hamburg, then later in Copenhagen during the late eighteenth century. While Zinck is remembered more perhaps for his flute and choral works than his keyboard music, this splendid Sonata does much to repay C. P. E.'s diligent teaching. This edition, made in 2011 by Christopher Hogwood, provides a welcome opportunity for pianists to revisit the music afresh, for it teems with surprises and yields many new insights into the period.

Initial difficulties lie in unpicking countless witty grace notes; subsequently, an appreciable level of dexterity will be required to bring off running passages on the modern instrument. Zinck evidently took great delight in piling on ever more unpredictable harmonic ideas, which result in some startling moments. Just when the home key of D minor is beginning to root itself in the development (bar 27) we are diverted without warning to E major at bar 49 – surely as brazen a tonal transgression as anything C. P. E. Bach might have shown him. Moments later, a sleight of hand par excellence returns us to the home key.

This music could work effectively on clavichord, fortepiano or even harpsichord, all of which retained the strongest advocacy during Zinck's time, although the bold dynamic markings might indicate a preference for the first two of these instruments. That said, only the supplest of fingers will successfully tease out the 'harpsichord' writing in places such as bars 17–21, and students will need to keep focused to dispatch the dramatic chordal cadences with confidence. The pace must be calculated to assimilate ornaments within semiquaver runs, but also to enable the triplets at bars 18–22 and 68–72 to fit tidily. An assertive broadening effect would seem idiomatic at Zinck's cheeky bridge passage at bars 49–57; elsewhere, students can be encouraged to find places to pause, albeit momentarily.

C:1 Miguel Astor Adriana

An entrancing waltz-like opening with a Latinesque rhythmic accompaniment and sensuous harmonies evokes the warm, passionate nature of a Venezuelan dance. It has a sweep and elegance in the outer sections, yet resembles film music in the middle section; here, abrupt changes of scene suggest agitated gossip, in a mixture of edgy, angular body language and ardent gestures.

The middle section is the most technically challenging. Bars 25–32 need to contrast the rhythmic precision and clear articulation of the LH chords with a more pliant and shapely melodic line. Voicing the LH to the top will help the brightness, and a blended legato enhances the string-like melody. The hands reverse roles in bars 33–9, demanding sophisticated control of the RH to convey clear yet unobtrusive accents and give rhythmic character above the vocal LH. The change of metre to a perceived two-in-a-bar in bars 40–41 should seem natural and be flexible enough to avoid a jolt to the flow. Bars 50–55 will rely on precision of balance in the RH 4ths, carefully judged to avoid any harshness in the passages marked *f*. Overall, 'slow-motion performance practice' – everything at a very moderate tempo, yet listening and responding musically – will improve the control.

Once the middle section's technical aspects have been mastered the outer sections will give it a musical context. Crucial to the visual image is a rhythmic flexibility and shaping of the melodic lines; time needs taking across some second beats, between phrases, and into some of the unexpected yet ravishing harmonies. A true finger legato throughout will enable students to adapt the timing of the pedal on unfamiliar pianos while preserving the legato line and conveying a warm sonority with harmonic clarity. A vivid range of colour will further draw in the audience, exploring the subtlest of *p* sonorities and voicing, especially towards the end where the waltz fades into a distant memory.

[C:2] **Brahms** Intermezzo in A minor

Brahms's reserved personality belies the profound and passionate communicator projected in his music. His compositions are always surprising, full of conflict between dark and light, and rich in their texture and harmonic language. Comparison with the sublime slow movement of his Violin Concerto will not only show this to students but engage them with Brahms's orchestration, an awareness of which will help in understanding the textural sophistication of his piano works.

The challenges here lie in subtlety of control and finesse of the 'orchestration' and phrases. Even the balance of the first RH chord, the beginning of a short melodic fragment in octaves with inner harmonies, will need very careful judgement. Voicing the chords to the top will allow for the quicker decay of the notes, and the bass note should add warmth and depth to the tone. From bar 8 the sobbing rests need to be communicated and yet the LH's arpeggiated accompaniment must still hold the root of the harmonies and avoid any intrusion. To this end the lower notes of the accompaniment should be held with the fingers, the pedal lifted for the rest and immediately reapplied as soon as the rest is observed. Coupling this with a gradual decrescendo as the arpeggio rises will keep the accompaniment subtly in the background.

The piece's dynamic range is subdued and yet colour and contrast is needed to keep the narrative alive. Carefully judged crescendos and diminuendos will be greatly enhanced by allowing more breadth of dynamic than the markings suggest. There should be a feeling of space and time throughout. Any forcing of the tempo or foreshortening of the rests will unsettle the music's personality. Longer phrases need to be kept in mind, avoiding too much rubato across short phrases, and the slowing of the pulse from the final *poco rit.* enables a longer, heart-rending silence before the final resigned and sorrowful restatement of the opening bars.

[C:3] **Peixun Chen** Selling Sundry Goods

This evocative, engaging piece is effectively a Cantonese folksong 'sandwich'; the outer sections are a set of variations on 'Selling Sundry Goods' while another song 'The Dressing Table' provides the contrasting middle section. The melodies sound related, since both rely on linked pentatonic scales, and the first melody works over the top of the second, albeit at half tempo. The sound of the Chinese zither is inherent in the articulation and notes, and familiarity with this timbre will greatly enhance interpretation.

Clarity, care with balance and an understanding of the underlying theme will draw the musical threads together. Memorizing the opening melody and then singing it over the top of the variations will give a clearer picture of the musical shape and direction and the clever, witty transformations. Sensitivity to balance is needed in bars 17 onwards where the RH accompaniment could

easily intrude; the semiquavers need a very light touch followed by a confident spring from the key surface to give a crisp chordal energy and rhythmic
precision. In the Con moto sections and at the end, uneven control of the
semiquavers will diminish the overall effect; a way to practise these is to
accent the offbeat notes with a fast finger (not a push), keeping all other
notes *pp*.

A lightness of touch and transparency of texture will communicate the opening, while a more bombastic, humorous *f* tone is needed in bars 12–16. The
middle section calls for a warmer, more pliant and pedalled approach.
Exaggerating each of the canonic melodies in turn from bars 50–61 will nurture the control for a musically responsive interpretation. The piece shouldn't
start too fast for there needs to be something in reserve for an impressive
finish from the final Allegro. The hand distribution in the last few bars works
well and allows a virtuosic flourish to the top followed by a short and decisive
final chord.

C:4 | Copland Jazzy

In this cheeky tilt-of-the-hat to the jazz idiom there is a humorous foxtrot in
the outer sections and a seductive, 'bluesy' middle section, all with a twist of
edgy Copland harmony. While looking relatively easy on the page, it demands
a relaxed physical freedom and control across the keys – and will benefit from
an extrovert presentation.

Rhythmic precision plays a major part in communicating the character of the
outer sections; to help this, much can be learnt in chords to encourage quick
hand positioning as the hands leap up the octaves. In bars 10 and 12, for
instance, both hands can play each triplet's notes as a chord to encourage a
confident jump. Using the LH rests to position the hand over the next notes in
advance helps accuracy and prepares the right, articulated sound. Bars 24–5
are much harder to read than play; memorizing the chords' chromatic movement will help confidence here. In the warmer-toned middle section, where
rhythmic pliancy will bring out the blues character, the top line of the RH
chords should be defined, and the LH's chromatic saxophone-like motifs
shaped and projected.

The opening may look fairly busy, but it is effectively a song, broken by chords
as if from the horn section. Since the first RH chord in bar 1 links melodically
to the middle C halfway through the bar, the intervening chordal flourishes
must be kept lighter. Similarly, the first melodic phrase ends at bar 3, and the
figurations which follow (like the triplets later on) are merely decoration.
Deciding what to project and what to keep out of the way will also suggest a
very clear pedalling – held through the first two beats of bars 1 and 5, for
instance. Precise counting of the rests is particularly important at the end,

both to ensure that the hands find the notes cleanly and to enhance the joke of the 'Tom and Jerry' finish.

[C:5] **Debussy** Doctor Gradus ad Parnassum

The rather dry instruction Clementi gives to one of his *Gradus ad Parnassum* exercises, *pour égaliser la force des doigts* (for developing equal finger strength), is tempered by Debussy's *égal et sans sécheresse*, clearly entreating a more musically engaged approach. Far from being a rigorous athletic event, this piece is instead a dreamlike world seemingly evoked in an effort to escape the dull repetition of semiquaver configurations. To play the piece well some considerable technical work will be needed, but it must never sound mechanical; a relaxed physiology coupled with a lightness of touch, delicacy of shape and sophistication of sonority, melodic line and pedal are needed from the start.

The hardest passage is bars 67–9, as the timing and brightness of the melodic B in the middle of the RH semiquavers may prove elusive. Slow practice nurturing the independence of sound on each note without pedal will put in the foundation; adding pedal will then demand greater contrast between the tune and accompanying semiquavers.

Of the many practising strategies to control the semiquavers elsewhere, the most useful is to accent alternate offbeat notes using solely finger speed while keeping the other notes *pp*; this helps students to acquire an even touch and develop independent tonal control in each finger. A key-surface touch is needed through the *pp* flourishes (e.g. in bars 9 and 10), delicate and not too articulated. The 'stems up' notes (bars 3–6 etc.) need clarity and subtle tonal control; staccato here merely implies projection. Rhythmic work in pairs and groupings will build an independent rhythmic control and a natural rubato. The middle D flat major section needs plenty of space and time, with careful judgement of tone in the bass note and voicing the LH 3rds as they go over the RH.

The best performances of this wonderful work will sound effortless and improvisatory, conveying an entrancing range of dynamic and tonal colour – far removed from the rigour of the composer Mozart called a 'mere mechanicus'.

[C:6] **Larsson** Allegro

This exciting work is almost like a film score in its rhythmic playfulness, contrasts and drama. It will need a committed, quick-witted and technically versatile performer who fearlessly navigates the keyboard, but the technical work required is so musically rewarded that few will resent the effort.

Rhythmic precision and character is at the heart, coupled with clarity of articulation. Familiarizing the rhythmic patterns into the fingers will work wonders. Clapping or tapping away from the piano, on a tabletop or on the piano lid, is useful; a rounded hand, using the ends of the fingers, will provide clarity to the rhythmic tap and assist the sound when returning to the keyboard. Using the appropriate fingering when doing this will also help in achieving consistent accuracy and fluency in the notes. Counting out loud while playing slowly will instil a firm sense of pulse, and, if coupled with expressive detail and articulation, will provide a confident template for building up tempo and giving a convincing interpretation.

Aside from rhythmic control, quick jumps across the keyboard are essential to fluency. 'Shadow jumping', quickly covering notes that follow, is invaluable in bars 15–20, 45–50 and particularly 55–9. This is best done at a slow tempo but with quick shifts of hand position, moving the moment the notes are released. Use of the sostenuto pedal, if available, might be considered in bar 39 to catch and sustain the LH F♯ octave.

 The work's energy and vibrancy will be all the more vivid with bold dynamic contrast and colour. Accents are bright and precise but not heavy, and pedal should be used sparingly in the faster passagework (except where pedal is implicitly suggested, in bars 55–9). A very soft *pp* is needed just towards the end with a well-judged and perhaps exaggerated *poco rit.* to set up the bold, forthright finish.

[C:7] **L. Berkeley** Prelude No. 5

 The quirky, irregular rhythms and contrast between humour and seriousness give this piece instant appeal. Its breezy, carefree character in the outer sections, with the sound-world somewhat reminiscent of a music box, juxtaposes sharply with the mixture of boldness and tenderness to be found midway. Impetus is created by the almost constant quaver movement, yet a broader feel of either two- or three-in-a-bar allows an energy and rhythmic attractiveness to the music.

 Different levels of tone will be needed for clarity in the three-stranded texture of the first section. A firm, quick attack, using a combination of fourth and fifth fingers, will add a brilliance to the melodic line in the opening bars, while sufficiently quiet inner notes will keep the texture free from confusion. Lateral movement, with the wrist relaxed, will create the flexibility needed for the widely spaced LH figures, and slow practice will ensure that the hands remain together. Memorizing the start of the middle section at bar 16 will enable your student to achieve precision in the leaps, especially in the LH. A light, bouncy hand touch will ensure that the octaves do not overpower the RH chords. Watching the thumb, and perhaps practising without the lower note, will help accuracy. Experimentation will reveal the most comfortable option for distribution between the hands of the widely spaced figuration in bars 65–6.

Sharply defined dynamic contrasts, often sudden, will give an immediacy to performance. A weighty f touch, in contrast to the brightness of the opening, adds grandeur to the middle-section chords, while a more yielding, relaxed mood seems to lower the temperature before the reprise of the opening music. Articulation details also play their part in highlighting rhythmic irregularity, especially in the middle section. Sparing use of pedal in short dabs will enhance harmonies at some points, but in general a drier texture seems to suit the mood.

C:8 Chopin Mazurka in A flat   (TB)

Chopin's Mazurkas, written throughout the composer's life, represent some of his most personal outpourings. In this late work he seems at times almost lost in his own world as he recalls the folk traditions of his native Poland. Dotted rhythms and accents create the spirit of the dance, while the mellow key of A flat major and rich harmonies evoke the elegance and sophistication of Paris, so beloved of this émigré composer. Much of the writing is straightforward for this level, but confident facility and bravura are needed for the more heroic sections.

Well-organized fingering will facilitate legato in the RH double notes. Placing a longer finger over the shorter fifth finger, a technique favoured by Chopin, may require slow practice, and initially isolating the upper line, playing with firm cantabile tone, will establish the melodic shape. Although the chromaticisms need a keen eye, especially the intricacies of bars 81–8, understanding their context is the best way to ensure they are consistently maintained. Confident LH leaps, isolating the larger movements, will lead to fluency, and a lateral swing towards the thumb will help the widely spaced arpeggiated chords.

Chopin described the pedal as 'the soul of the piano'. Here it plays a dual role in sustaining bass notes, thereby conveying the harmonic structure, and in enriching the texture. The ear will best judge how much pedal to use, and how frequently to change it. Incisive dotted rhythms and the rhythmic displacement caused by accents on second and third beats, which vary according to their context, are characteristic features of the mazurka. Imagining this folk-inspired dance performed by different groupings of dancers may provide a vivid picture for the clearly defined sections, each with their own distinct tonal and rhythmic character. Particularly striking moments are the boldness of the f at bar 23, with its filled-out texture, and the brief appearance of melody in the LH at bar 69.

[C:9] Gershwin Liza ⓉⒷ

🎹 The juicy harmonies and rich pianistic texture of this delicious song transcription capture perfectly the elegance and sophistication of the 1920s. Two main sections, major followed by minor, form the structure, each of which is repeated with variations in the figuration. Gershwin has provided many specific musical directions, yet in the end the freedom and spontaneity of an after-dinner entertainment, as if improvised for a group of friends, will lie at the heart of a convincing performance. Although ideal for a student with a large stretch, the piece is accessible to most players if the occasional inner note in chords is omitted and there is good flexibility for the 'stride bass'.

✋ Initially practising in strict time, placing each note precisely on its 'time-spot', is a good starting point from which to explore a more flexible approach. The pedal is essential for catching both notes in the LH 10ths at the opening and subsequently, whereas its use elsewhere is dictated by phrasing and articulation. Creative ways of breaking down the texture into its constituent parts will help to unravel any complexities, and playing each note of chords in arpeggio fashion will make the ear aware of harmonies. Leaps are dependent on freedom of arm movement, with the more athletic bars probably requiring memorizing.

🎨 Listening to a recording of the original song, perhaps the version by Judy Garland, will give a feel for phrasing and changes of mood. The composer distinguishes between accents and tenuto marks, both of which contribute to the rhythmic character. Arm weight will produce the warmth of tone to convey the languid feel at the opening, in contrast to the firmer, brighter attack needed for the variant at bar 33. The legato octave melody at bar 17, consisting of two four-bar phrases, is punctuated by more detached chords; your student should note that this tune is concealed beneath a countermelody at its subsequent reappearance at bar 49.

[C:10] Medtner Idylle ⓉⒷ

🎹 The title suggests a dreamlike state, perhaps a daydream, an atmosphere magically evoked in this beautiful piece. Its spirit of Russian melancholy is somewhat akin to that of Rachmaninov, a compatriot and near contemporary, yet the very chromatic melodic figuration is highly individual. Imagination and flexibility are needed to capture the music's ebb and flow, and a keen awareness of the pedal's dual role – in creating sonority as well as sustaining harmonies – will capture the sound-world of this late-Romantic idiom.

✋ The frequent use of accidentals may be daunting at first, but further inspection will reveal that the figuration is made up largely of chromatic scale patterns. However, care should be taken to maintain accidentals through the bar, especially in LH chords, and distinguishing between ties and slurs is dependent on a keen eye. The ear will dictate the frequency of pedal changes. The pedal is often relied on to sustain bass notes, especially in the widely spaced arpeggios in bars 34 and 36, whereas at times frequent pedal changes will be needed to filter out chromatic clashes.

Overlapped fingers, as if reluctant to release the keys, will produce a suitably suave, ultra-smooth tone for the figuration. The LH opening quaver motif underpins the piece, forming the basis for a broad melodic outline. In the RH, additional arm weight and sensitive balancing of the surrounding notes will highlight the melodic notes, indicated by the double stems. Your student can enjoy the cross-rhythms, which occasionally throw off balance the two-in-a-bar lilt, enhancing the intangible mood. There are two climax points, the second of which will have an almost overwhelming effect if the three ingredients of crescendo (starting from *pp*), accelerando, and shortening of note values to triplets are well judged. The calmness of the coda which follows at Tempo I serves as a reminder that all is well in what is merely a dream.

C:11 Mendelssohn Song without Words (TB)

The *moto perpetuo* style of this piece from the much-loved collection of *Songs without Words* will appeal to a student with well-developed fingers and plenty of natural facility. It is sometimes known by the nickname 'The Bee's Wedding', but its more familiar title 'Spinning Song', added by the composer or his circle after initial publication, conjuring up an image of home life in the nineteenth century, is probably more helpful. The scherzo-like character so familiar in many of Mendelssohn's works, perhaps here suggesting the ceaseless motion of a spinning wheel powered by treadle action, is perfectly evoked, and the composer's superb command of piano writing is apparent throughout.

Clear fingerwork with a regular pulse is an essential starting point. Occasional checking with a metronome, gradually increasing the tempo, will alert your student to any discrepancies in pace. A crisp attack from the finger, assisted by slight rotation of the hand, will give clarity to the melodic lines woven into the figuration, while keeping close to the keys will aid control of the inner accompanying notes. In addition, lateral wrist movement will assist the more widely spaced figures. Slow practice is invaluable for synchronization, especially when semiquavers shift between hands, and silently shadowing the inner notes will provide the physical sensation of distinguishing melody from accompaniment. Students with small hands might explore redistributing the wider LH stretches between the hands, or, if necessary, omitting the thumb notes.

Thinking in two-in-a-bar, lightening offbeat notes, will give grace to the rhythmic character, thereby offsetting any possible monotony created by the constant semiquaver motion. Charm and delicacy of tone pervade much of the piece, yet surges in tone, often followed by a *subito p*, add excitement and colour. The *ff* climax, featuring augmented 6th harmony, serves as a focal point. Further harmonic surprises can be highlighted by momentary dabs of pedal and slurred quaver couplets provide variety from the predominantly staccato touch.

C:12 **Paderewski** Nocturne   TB

Here is an exquisite little-known gem whose nuanced and expressive character will appeal to a sensitive student. The fine keyboard writing, which explores both a wide range of the piano and the expressive qualities of the pedal, confirms Paderewski's important standing in the piano world of the early twentieth century. While the style of the piece owes much to Chopin, the perfumed harmonies and heartfelt mood place it firmly in the tradition of salon pieces. The dreamlike outer sections of its ternary structure, with their soaring melodic lines, sandwich more impassioned music midway. Here the cello-like LH lines, later joined in dialogue by the RH, drive forward towards an impassioned, albeit short-lived climax.

Creating perfectly matched joins between the hands is likely to be the main challenge in the outer sections. Experimentation will discover the most comfortable posture for moving the LH swiftly and effortlessly across the keyboard. Unwanted bumps in tone can be prevented by arriving at new positions in advance of playing, and organized fingering is needed to sustain ties. The responsiveness of the pedal may be different on an unfamiliar exam piano. Strong harmonic foundations are conveyed by sustaining important bass notes but, as always, careful listening will ensure that the pedal releases fully on all changes of chord.

Slowly exploring the harmonies, luxuriating in the subtlety of the shifts, is a good starting point for understanding the musical language. The chords offer scope for sensitive voicing, for instance giving prominence to the tenor line in bar 1, while offbeat accents and double-dotted rhythms heighten the expression in the outer sections. The gentlest cantabile lines, supported by a sensitively balanced accompaniment, convey the calm atmosphere here, especially when enhanced by the *una corda* pedal for the final bars, whereas the middle section, with its sense of urgency as a variety of keys are discovered, needs more robust sonorities and firmly projected lines for full effect.

C:13 **Poulenc** Improvisation No. 7 in C   MT

Poulenc's intoxicating sound-world is placed into broader context by Milhaud, Honegger and the other members of Les Six – a sophisticated coterie of Parisian composers who enjoyed nothing more than meeting in restaurants to discuss music, poetry and painting. Partly in reaction to the Impressionism of Debussy and Ravel, but also to the extravagances of Wagner and the German Romantic movement, there sprang music born of an edgier, more piquant and aromatic language. Ancient, rustic French folk melodies merged imperceptibly into jazz and music-hall tunes to form the basis for memorable character pieces. An unmistakable quirkiness emerged, which was idealistically perhaps closer to Toulouse-Lautrec's ironic paintings than, say, Monet's colourful creations.

Rubato implications here are carefully notated using familiar French directions, such as *cédez* (bars 13, 28 and 33) and *animez peu à peu* (bar 23). However, beginning daily practice by simply playing through the entire melody in isolation, passing seamlessly between the hands at bars 18, 23 and 30, should illuminate further prospects for subtle inflection. From bar 10 the RH must divide its resources to accommodate accompanimental textures, which surely presents the chief technical challenge. Apart from four centrally positioned bars (25–8) the dynamic level never exceeds *mf*; indeed, the 'bright' key of C major calls for a restrained, sunny charm – nothing too emphatic or unmediated, even in the strenuous *fff* octave declamation at bar 28.

Music which is improvised – as Classical concerto cadenzas once were – contrasts markedly with that which exudes an improvisatory air (Schubert's Impromptus, for example), and could prove a useful discussion point. As Count Basie once mused, 'the best improvisations are well rehearsed.' Students should therefore grapple decisively with Poulenc's assiduous markings before wading in with ideas of their own. For this 'miniature' to sound improvised it can tolerate flexibility, though anecdote has it that the composer became enraged by pianists who indulged in too much rubato and pedal.

C:14 Rachmaninov Daisies

Rachmaninov ranks among the finest pianist-composers. During his lifetime his popularity was not as consistently high as would seem conceivable, given the man's extraordinary capacity for lyricism, intense romanticism and bell-like Impressionism. Even after taking up residency in America he remained determined to rejuvenate the Russia he had known and loved before the Revolution. From works as comprehensively challenging as his third piano concerto to the briefest of vignettes, such as *Daisies*, the whole keyboard is regularly required. Rachmaninov's massive hands (he could stretch a 13th) encouraged him to create quasi-orchestral effects on the piano, and yet never is a note squandered out of tasteless bravura.

Accompanimental figures are rarely predictable in Rachmaninov's music. The LH's humble-looking semiquaver motion will repay careful isolated practice, with pedal, to ensure nothing is missed. Not unlike Chopin's fioritura, the RH figurations at bars 5, 29 and 31 need to sound as cool as a mountain stream. Subdividing the notes in an attempt to match up with the LH will prove profitless; it will be better to permit these an independent life of their own, though placing finger 4 on the B♭ in the first two instances, and then thumb on the E in the last (as it tumbles out of the trill), should hasten the learning process somewhat.

Rubato is so bound up in Rachmaninov's writing that pianists frequently overstep the mark in a bid to stamp their own personalities. The longest phrases possible should be targeted here, for Rachmaninov was a supreme tunesmith. Encourage your student to look for chances to enjoy a singing LH thumb and to treasure the deliciously circumspect climax at bars 18–21. It is just as well there is a *rit.* just before this moment, to ease the subterranean LH D♭ at bar 18 – even students with smaller hands can afford to take their time in reaching up for the A♭ that follows.

[C:15] Ravel Menuet

The sombre backdrop to Ravel's *Le Tombeau de Couperin* (composed to commemorate six friends who died during World War I) belies the surprisingly optimistic charm of the suite as a whole. Though he acknowledged François Couperin, Ravel actually modelled the work on the Baroque French suite's more generic sensibilities. 'Menuet' – the penultimate piece from the suite – makes play of a delightfully limpid melody. Though both Debussy and Ravel contested the term 'Impressionism', it remains a partly helpful means of expressing the sound-world of their music. One can see why Ravel orchestrated the suite, for its multiplicity of effects and registral changes leaves open boundless possibilities, some of which can gainfully inform pianists.

Notes bearing both staccatos and slurs are not so much contradictions in terms as clues to the technique best suited to the effect the composer was after; in this context the effect will be entirely influenced by deft pedalling throughout. Amid so much quiet playing, any tendency to dilute the all-important top-note melody should be avoided, especially in the thickly textured chords at bars 41–8. While Ravel's indications invite careful weighing up regarding *una corda* pedal (*Sourdine*), he does not always notate '3 cordes'; it might be prudent to add this at bar 81.

A tempo of around ♩ = 104 would encourage an unhurried dispatch, one which accords integrity to the minuet form – a dignified, rather popular dance in the eighteenth century. Students can seize all opportunities to be expressive, but never at the risk of rhythmic inexactness. There are two conspicuous regions to home in on dynamically – the **ff** at bar 57 and **f** at bar 111. Intriguingly, at the beginning of bar 41 Ravel's punctilious phrasing renders the score a serpent-like appearance; this marks a moment of special translucence, an opportunity to inject a new, perfumed quality.

[C:16] **Edwin Roxburgh** Moonscape

Roxburgh's highly accessible contemporary piano pieces make use of intricate textures and timbres – the music is consistently pianistic, but never self-indulgent. *Moonscape*, composed in 1995, is divinely ambient in idiom; it will undoubtedly intrigue your more thoughtful, colouristically aware student. The music trickles ruminatively out of faintly disturbing Messiaen-like chords, though its frequent changes of time signature are usually more a way of flagging up subtly altering emphases than distinctive divisions of metre. Importantly, therefore, a quaver pulse must be encouraged to underpin the music throughout, suggesting the moon's heartbeat perhaps, quickening only briefly at bars 38–9.

Bars 6–8, 11–13 and 41–2 are bitonal – black notes in the LH, white in the RH; here the aim is to gently 'ping out' the upwardly beamed melodic strands with fourth and fifth fingers. The throbbing pulse at bars 17–21 and 32–7 deserve the subtlest coaxing out, while the 'distant' moments at bars 27 and 41 probably warrant *una corda* pedal. An early moon-burst to f at bar 8 proves to be one of only three such isolated markings in the entire score, but students should take care to voice the LH firmly at bars 14–17. Bars 27–32 imply wide LH stretches, but students should fear not: *Ped. sempre* saves the day.

The *sotto voce*, dolce and cantabile markings which liberally punctuate the score, alongside further indications in English, encourage microscopic attention to detail and the most feathery of touches. The invitation to *laissez vibrer* in those 'timeless' bars 38–9 should be enjoyed. Once the three-against-twos here have been perfected, they should be tucked away to be barely noticeable – as if shimmering rays of light beamed deep into the Milky Way. Unlike Debussy, who intriguingly did not mark in pedal effects despite their indispensability in much of his music, Roxburgh gives thorough and specific indications, which require full assimilation or else the music will lose its poetic verve.